MAN-HANDLED

By the same author:

Perfectly Bruised (bilingual Mandarin + English selected) (2019)
Goodbye, Cruel (2017)
Drag down to unlock or place an emergency call (2013)
First..., Then... (2012)
Mapless in Underland (2004)
Pushing thirty, wearing seventeen (2001)

(with Caren Florance):
Listen, bitch (poetry + art book) (2019)
Members Only (poetry + art book) (2017)
1962: Be Spoken To (artist book) (2017)

MAN-HANDLED

MELINDA SMITH

Man-handled
Recent Work Press
Canberra, Australia

Copyright © Melinda Smith, 2020

ISBN: 9780648834335 (paperback)

 A catalogue record for this book is available from the National Library of Australia

All rights reserved. This book is copyright. Except for private study, research, criticism or reviews as permitted under the Copyright Act, no part of this book may be reproduced, stored in a retrieval system, or transmitted in any form by any means without prior written permission. Enquiries should be addressed to the publisher.

Cover image: Neil Roberts, *The Space Inside My Fist*, 1995, 9.8 x 3.4 x 3.4 cm (irreg.). Lead crystal edition of 20 created by Luna Ryan at Canberra Glassworks in 2017, cast from terracotta original. Photograph: David Paterson. © Neil Roberts/Copyright Agency, 2020. Reproduced with permission.

Cover design: Recent Work Press
Set by Recent Work Press

Melinda Smith acknowledges the support of artsACT in writing this book.

Supported by

recentworkpress.com

PL

Contents

Manifest   1

Exposures

Afternoon at La Pietra   5
Stendhal syndrome   6
Tulsi teabag found at the bottom of my laptop case   7
Past perfect   8
In the Garden of Succulents, Changi Airport, Terminal One   9
Interrupting the bread-making   10
A history in six dishes   11
bare   13

The space inside his fist

his heart on the outside   17
The space inside his fist   18
The Dude Abides   20
Ty-Reisha, Liri, Narciso   22
Roost   23
eyelashes   24
#tfw   25
Post-Game   26
Orion as a woman unhelped by White Ribbon   27

Listen, bitch

Ernie Ecob as a Bare-Bellied Joe   33
Sweetheart,   34
Zero Sum   35
Simmer down   37
GO AWAY   39
There does come a time   40
Folly   41
I do not permit a woman to teach   42
Solving the problem   43
Strong Advice   45
Don Burke's Statement — 26 November 2017   47
Total Fabrication   50

Two-hole blues 52
supreme gentleman 53
only fair 54
Eurydice's Last Sky 55

The Night Book

mothful 59
Tree no. 7, Haig Park, Canberra 60
Last thoughts at the Shoalhaven 61
Jazz quartet 63
Bloodnut Gut-wrench 65
Deru Kui 66
Michael Collins 67
Julia after Tony's boning 68
Ba   by Joy 69
DIY Empire 70
22 November 2018 71

Fugal States

Fugal state 75
Apes rule 77
red, white and window 78
in/sight 79
like anything 80
Some assembly required 81
Marks 83
Newcastle reckoning 86

Ventriloquies

Two poems by Sulpicia 91
Pairs 92
Map of the peninsula 93
Welcome Home 94
Sweet nothing 96
21 buttons for Yoshiko 包み釦二十一個 97

Afterword 104

Manifest

If you must make me,
draw me forth through that
needle's eye

have a care for this raw skin
what abrades it, how
it may be sliced and sutured

I was pure electricity, pure simian ululation
If you must cage me
box and bottle me

franken-birth me
in a clumsy bucket
you will learn the sorrow of mangle and botch

of the warp and the scorch mark

You will see it is no sorrow

With luck I may multiply

I may layer, matrix, palimpsest
I may go choral, become geology
Take your hand from me

set me among a swarm of eyes
As they move over me
they will mark me, too

EXPOSURES

Afternoon at La Pietra

Someone has silk-stockinged the sun.
Every yellow villa wall is a spread net
of marigold. For afternoons like this,

marble is hewn and placed as an offering;
a creamy glowline flares along a pale brow,
a marvel of cheekbone; a spread palm

cups its blessing of radiance. For afternoons like this,
words like *burnish* and *mellow* are required,
are called into being. Words like *worship*.

Do not say them yet.
Stand a moment in the late gold day.
Look upon the rock, the brick, the carved, the uncarved,

taking their bright, slant benediction. See and stay silent, see
stone itself anointed and caused to speak,
blindingly eloquent with light.

Stendhal syndrome

Swooning is so 1817. But I can say truthfully, it happened,
        this century, in the Uffizi. It *happened*.

Tears, even. I know. I thought
        I was past that. I thought we all were.

Everyone cringes at words like *transport*,
        ecstasy. I was drunk, your honour, drunk on paint -

no, drunk on charcoal and paper,
        those only. Or the echo of prayer. Struck

dumb and ringing like a cuffed head, a bell,
        a gong, trembling, concussed, a pulsing

tuning fork, thrumming the same note
        as all the others, overcome by the marks of the master's

hand, this last sketch too much, the straw, just
        grey and black on yellowed paper, just perfect

love, caught, still breathing, one radiant face
        among thousands, *full-on*   felling me   still

Tulsi teabag found at the bottom of my laptop case

So light, it exerts no pressure on the palm
Like holiness   Like the idea of holiness

It is not a permanent solution to anything
yet it waits, an unworn cardigan of quiet

Its skin is bleached elephant: buff-coloured,
soiling to brown at the edges—a small rag

rescued from the dust   It smells of dried apple
and the sweetness of ink   It bears the bruises

of neglect, the soft creases of patience
It cradles its flimsy gift, its mixed blessings

and blossoms in the scald of water

Past perfect

You were always receding   That day
there was sun striking the rocks

You crossed, smiled back
Too late, I snapped you

In the picture you blur, turning,
your toe grazing the skin of the creek

It still feels like nothing—
the blue-white milk tears

welling from a pulled weed
or water warming on a leaf,

slick and disappearing
Even the fine hairs lie down

and will not tickle
You were always a *had-been*

—not petrichor, not portent,
but the air drying, after rain;

light, refocusing itself
returning from lace to window

In the Garden of Succulents, Changi Airport, Terminal One

You and I enter by the *Barrel Cactus*, and stand
too close to each other at the bar. Two beers,
some conversation, some digs at the flight
we have just endured—we can do this, we have

an air-traffic-controller's view of pink afternoon clouds,
of the *Siamese Sago Palm*, the *Indian Spurge*, the *Moses
-in-the-Cradle*. Labels state their origins and habits.
Being ROOFTOP and OPEN AIR, smokers also grow here,

and giant umbrellas, taut and beige, and sunburned ladies,
with equally taut foreheads, who are painting their nails.
There are no labels for their origins or habits. We search
for an explanation of the foot-long spikes atop the umbrellas.

We agree some mysteries will have to remain here, when we
board our onward flights. The *Ponytail Tree* makes us laugh
a little too much. There are frangipani over by the wall,
the blossoms shading from palest shell-pink, through hussy-pink,

to insistent purple. We cross the courtyard to admire them,
continue on the shaded path, past *Moss Rose*, *Desert Rose*,
Carpet Rose. Dragonflies, in tiny holding patterns, take
the sunset's blush. We stop behind the *Rose Cactus*. You move

closer. I notice the *Devil's Tongue*. And the *Devil's Bone*. You press
me against you. You are blocking my air-traffic controller's view.
I see chest, and sideburns, and feel the sting in my nostrils
of the clashing designer perfumes we have been spraying on each other

in the Duty Free. There are many labels for this, most of them
too flattering. I dash late to my boarding call, refusing to friend you
on Facebook. On the way out of course I see the *Burn Plant*.
The *Bayonet Plant*, the *Crown of Thorns*. Last of all, too late, I spot

the sign: a black and white cartoon, a red slashed circle, the words
DON'T TOUCH

Interrupting the bread-making

The frost has woken her early
She pads into the freezing kitchen
in her hand-me-down quilted dressing-gown
sniffing the yeasty air
She is discovering for the first time
her father's secret early-morning life
Almost younger than words,
she can only stroke solemnly
the ears of the knitted rabbit
cradled in her arm
and watch as her father
clapping flour from his grey hands
wrenches open the door of the pot-bellied stove,
prods a roaring orange monster mouth
with a dark metal wand
There are nuggets inside, blurred with flame
They flare and settle, the mouth
spits little pellets of grey
onto the hearthstone
like biscuit crumbs, like bread crumbs
She reaches for them, too late
the air is full of loud
and from that moment
the word *No* is black and orange and ash,
is the sound of skin sizzling,
is the texture of a puckered fingertip,
and *Don't touch* somehow smells
like coking coal and yeast and father, and
curiosity, stubbornness, defiance
sting like bare feet on a winter morning,
chafe like coarse wool
dig like a dressing-gown cord
pink, frayed, tied too tight—
a cord which is not umbilical
but which is, nevertheless
a species of tether

A history in six dishes

First, apple-crumble topping: chunks of butter, brown sugar,
cinnamon, mixed spice, rubbed in,
thumb against fingertips, rubbed and rubbed in,
like sweet wet sand
rasping the skin
until clumping in rolling crumbs.
This to stand for my mother, and baking,
and hot-dessert-days which were always occasions,
and learning these things from her.

Next, cold turkey slices with canned cranberry sauce,
served simply, on rye bread or similar.
This to stand for our orphan Christmas
in DC, just the two of us, and for me
deciding, in that white-out northern winter,
that when we returned
to our own dry highland
it would be time to have your children.

Oblong slices of haloumi cheese, toasted
in the sandwich maker, done until straw-coloured,
no darker; a single leaf of fresh basil
atop each one.
These to stand for the care the new mother
must take of herself: salty, nourishing,
high in protein and calcium—even containing greens—
and able to be prepared
in three scant minutes.

Figs, pale green,
soft and slightly pleated, ample-bottomed,
warm from the tree, milk still oozing
from where they have been twisted off the stem.
These to stand for our old house, where
we nearly ended, where
the gorgeous Sicilian White
flourished in the swampy back yard
despite our neglect, filling, every February,
with sugar-mad wattle birds.

Chicken breasts, browned on the striped hotplate,
then roasted with olive oil and rosemary
on a bed of carrots, cauliflower,
potato—or all three.
All of the foods our eldest would eat, in one dish,
served almost every night, for years.
These to stand for the way
I had to learn to start again with him, how
he taught me what he needed,
piece by piece, how it was different, but
not un-beautiful.

Finally, brussels sprouts, roasted with garlic and bacon
until charred and oozing, until
they sit in small sweet pools
of their own delicious damage.
These to stand for my discovering,
after sixteen years,
that there were still foods
I didn't know you loved.

bare

The dead are necessary   they are forked like
branches   they have their own names   call them:

they are not hiding   what use will you come to?
a eucalypt stag   a roost, a burrow, a rooting-place

great grey bones and a shiver of weed   ants
will forage in your shoes   shaken out

they will come back   and back
                              I went
to the mountain   she gave me three no-things:

a eucalypt sprig   just born but fallen,   pink-twigged,
sprouting little poked-tongue buds   of acid-yellow

a tiny stop-motion spider   teleporting   from one dead leaf
to another   all the brown sickle shapes   maps

of the same country   the wind of the turning year
that sky-deep   irresistible shove
                              I went

to the mountain   showed her my bare feet
my no-feet   tucked under too long on the blanket

waxy, cracked like pale stone, weathered, split,
cross-hatched   dusty with dead cells   she laid claim

rising   I turned back   a prickling of blood   ants
warring   between pink-twigged   tarsal bones

this gait, this no-gait   jittering, contingent   a shiver of weed
a eucalypt   fallen   a claim   a forked question   of use

THE SPACE INSIDE HIS FIST

his heart on the outside

he wishes
it were armoured   he is always afraid of being
kicked in it

it still speaks
to him   but he has unlearned its language—soft,
nestled, veined

syllables
he cannot catch   he likes to give it slightly more space
than it

actually needs
facing any kind of reckoning, he shields it and will not
be answerable

he persists
in thinking that in its default state, limp, indifferent, it is
of the slightest

interest
whatsoever   when it stirs, unfurls, fills with sap   it is magnificent
but still

only potentially
important   it is only when he surrenders it   yields it up   that it can change
anything at all

it must bloom, mutely,
in a small pocket of disputed territory   like a trumpet-flower, a marrow-blossom,
like a bound wound

unwinding

as a

white

flag

The space inside his fist

(after a glasswork by Neil Roberts / Luna Ryan 1995/2017,
lead crystal, cast from terracotta original, edition of 20,
9.8x3.4x3.4 (irreg))

i.

A play-doh hand-grab,
saved and made solid;
a Nude, a more-than-Nude:
a palpable x-ray of flesh-wrapped space

Skinnier at one end,
where the thumb wraps;
ribbed; softly faceted
at the inner knuckle-folds

The callouses showing
like little craters:
it is a small sausage
pitted with work

It lies, on its bare plinth,
a heavy handful of nothing,
puny, vulnerable, a petrified
snail, shelled   helpless

ii.

Not one noun, but many—as many as there are fists
to close This is what the rope knows of the sailor,
what the oar knows of the sculler what the caught fly

knows, one time in a hundred, what the middy knows
of the drinker   what the door-handle knows of the one
who enters what the long hair of the victim knows

what her arms and shoulders know also what the stock
of the shotgun knows, and the edge of the dragged
blanket   what the shovel knows of the digger of holes,

what the steering-wheel knows,
ten and two.

The Dude Abides

'What makes a man? Is it doing the right thing?
—Sure, that and a pair of testicles'
—The Big Lebowski, 1998 film by Joel and Ethan Coen

How to hold each other
straight man to straight man
frail and tender on a sea cliff

You have no frame of reference here Donny
as the wind covers you both
in the ashes of your friend

How to mourn *like a child*
who wanders in in the middle of a movie
the mud-sunk faces of the war

How to make your way, your
strikes and gutters, ups and downs
ins, outs, what-have-yous, all the while

watching the guy in the next lane
Strong men also cry. Strong men also cry
How not to believe in precisely nothing

How to make a place to return to
to become clean and whole
a place to best and be bested

according to immutable rules
How to cover your soft crotch
against the savage marmot,

the scissor-wielding nihilist,
the artist whose work is highly vaginal
How to enter a world of pain

whilst preserving the integrity
of your beverage How not
to treat objects like women

How not to have a stranger
mark your territory with his urine
or fuck you in the ass

How to tie the room together

Ty-Reisha, Liri, Narciso

si se non noverit
—Ovid, Metamorphoses, Book III, 316-510

Narciso leans over, neck bending deep like a pale stem, stock still,
staring into a small square pool in his palm, hour by hour,
stroking its glass face. It buzzes softly with moon's light, hums with
infinite schools of brash fish, ripples that will not stop, that
carry to the lip of consequence. He cradles it, gazes
as the thickening weeds reach up for him, green arms dripping

I came to leave his food
this morning he was just
gone, his phone abandoned
I scrolled through   He'd been
chatting with some woman called
Eko   on Tindr There were A LOT
of selfies My poor boy That fortune-teller,

years ago — 'Ty-Reisha', was it? —
warned me   *Liri, you best pray*
that child never know hisself,
just sayin' Every weary day since,
I have carried that massing burden
Today I know its full weight
I can drop it; take up

my cleansing wail
                    Beside
the phone, the plate
with yesterday's leftovers;
sprouting from the heel
of bread, a small, perfect
flower, some kind of daffodil

dangling itself at the screen

Roost

He settles at the table
Pale eyes, baleful
DAAAAAHN'T, DAAAAAHN'T
he cries, when pressed
for any explanation

These ones come home too,
you know—these furtive ravens
This one here will home
and home, he will nest
with his rusted panel van

in your front yard, fag packets
strewing the lawn   His familiar,
the blue cattle dog, will howl
and howl, enacting this long
tethering, a collar of old rope

lashed to wheel-less axle
You had thought that,
fledged, he would fly
and fly   He was equipped
only to dumpster-dive

and boomerang   He settles
at the table, plumage dark
and greasy   Scrapes his chair
Nips another fag from the packet
with thin fingers, spreads his

awkward shoulders, coughs
Refused a light, he shudders;
huffs   *FAAAAHHHHHK YOU*
The pale eyes leak   He glares
and glares, and slumps, stropping
his beak   on your peace

eyelashes

She remembers Matt-from-down-the-road. She remembers his uncle's panel-van, parked on the street in front of his house; the car body's dull red, the rust-spots on the driver's door. Remembers sitting talking to Matt in the back of the van; its brown carpet, its wet-dog, engine-oil smell. Remembers the uncle crossing the yard, hopping into the van, sitting cross-legged in ripped jeans, lighting up a Winfield Blue; his white-blond hair, his white eyelashes, almost invisible; him chatting, asking questions. She does not remember crossing her own legs, her shorts gaping, showing candy-striped underpants. She does remember the uncle reaching out, his jabbing finger, him slipping it inside the fabric, deft, practised. Him grinning *better not sit like that, or that's what'll happen* Her face hot, then cold; Matt and the uncle giggling; her dizziness; her silently-closing legs; her sense that around her there had descended a small fug of shame. She remembers that dull red feeling, its stink of engine oil, wet dog, Winfield Blues. Does not remember how many years it stayed.

#tfw

There is a sonnet walking toward you
like a man at an airport, like a stranger
from Adelaide who wants to connect with you
on LinkedIn He is stalking toward you He says
WYD? I want to add you to my network
   wid There is work, walking toward a sonnet *wide*
There is a link in the net *weed* There is
an airport at Adelaide stranger than a man
You are leaving the sonnet What are you
doing? You are returning to the sea Your feelings are wide-
summer-holiday-carsickness feelings
seven hours staring through a glass
triangle edged with black rubber
You are returning a glass triangle to the sea

The glass triangle returns the sea to you
and the sea returns your feelings, with weed
for seven hours Your black rubber holiday
Your carsick summer The feeling sea
is stalking toward you, swiping
at linked sonnets You will never connect
with the black rubber net from Adelaide airport,
with the wide carsick man, with the seven
summer triangles You are walking on strange glass.
There is an edge, feeling toward a man, returning
to the want. He says I work to weed you
why are you leaving? You swipe
at the rubber stalker, at the black summer
      There is a net that returns

Post-Game

It is always the same hotel room—Kobe—Capetown—
on the wall, a bad watercolour   A harbour scene   ships coming in

The same room, the same grey bedspread—Palmerston North—Randwick—
the same mini bar   never enough milk for White Russians   This bothers him

They won tonight   The fizz of it in him   They are all here together, jostling,
baying   the whole forward line   musky, swarming round the bed,

spilling drinks on the grey   The lamp is tilted just a little, the left-hand
bed-lamp, listing   It has a dent at the base that looks like a witch's face

The watercolour is badly hung, not quite level   This bothers him   He wonders
about the girl on the bed   lying diagonally across the corner   He wonders

why he is here   bonding   The ships jitter in their frame   This bothers him
Teams can be strange things   The curtains are almost transparent   He wonders

about swarming, and musk, and how old she is   The big prop, the one
they call Beast, grasps her pony-tail, manoeuvres her head   They are

coming in   the ships   all at once   swarming on a king tide   This
bothers him   He wonders why she is here   with her pony-tail   why

she is always here   with the ships in their bad water, the dented face,
the bedspread, listing   Beast finishes, pulls out of her mouth   He wonders

about things done badly   about winning, fizzing   about how it is never
enough   She sinks face down   almost transparent   He stops wondering:

not that old   The pile of team jerseys slides from the bedspread to the floor
This bothers him   The witch face   still watching   from under the light

Orion as a woman unhelped by White Ribbon

(Rigel)
    Not everyone
    in the sky
    is there because
    they won
    Bitch left him
    —bad idea bitch—

(Saiph)
    He tracked her
    to the shopping centre,
    watched the sliding doors
    part their glass to admit her
    and her trolley,

(Hatsya)
    scrambled
    under her car,
    waited   heard her
    return, heard her
    heft the bags
    into the boot
    waited

    heard her
    opening the driver's side,
    moved, rolled, rose,
    took aim, before
    she could close
    the door

    saw her wide eyes,
    saw her turn, too late,
    the bullet shattering her
    left thigh, watched her
    double over, gone
    pale, gone

(Mintaka)
blue-white
with the thought: her child
in her belly, there,
jutting above the seatbelt,
heard her

(Alnilam)
scream at him,
keep screaming,
stop
They arrested him
but like he said,
she had it coming

(Alnitak)
He was out in five
She's in the sky now
easiest to see in summer;
blue-white all over
left leg still
blood-red

(Bellatrix)
and there, above the seatbelt,
her baby crying out inside her
Its tears bead and glitter;
three of them
drop down

(Meissa)
Every October she rains,
little traumas, falling
into the spring night,
falling as meteors
We ignore them

(Betelgeuse)
Any year now
her wound-star will go
nova—already 8th brightest
in the sky, when it is re-born, not even
the sun will blot it, we'll see it
wherever we go,
all day, all night
long

LISTEN, BITCH

Ernie Ecob as a Bare-Bellied Joe

Women only want to be shearers for the sex
—Ernie Ecob, former Secretary, Australian
Workers' Union[1]

She takes me by my hind legs, which are
my only legs   *Women want for shearers*

to be the only sex   Looks through me,
intent, a pack face seeing a herd face

Sex be for shearers. To the women,
only want   Slides me into position,

grasping her machinery   *To be women,*
only sex the shearers for want   the teeth

glint, the dark comb   dangling   *Shearers*
want sex only to be for the women   I kick

and stumble   *Sex be for women.*
To the shearers, only want   —bleating—

glory if she gets me   *Shearers only want*
to be women for the sex   If I hold still

she might not draw blood   this time
Women want the shearers to only be

for sex   I freeze and brace, my sheep eyes
blanking   blow by blow   she peels me

After, nearly fleeceless, spent, I feel her
bend, take me in gentle headlock, lips

in my white ear   Her low growl: 'Women,
Ernie, women—women *only want*   to be.'

Sweetheart,

you don't need a model
to work this one out[2]   If you take out
uncovered
meat
and place it outside on the street
and the cats come and eat it
whose fault is it, the cats
or the uncovered meat?[3] The GST
will greatly affect the workers of Australia
and their wives[4] hairy legged
femocrats[5] they will abort
a baby just because it is
inconvenient or summer is approaching
and they want to wear a bikini[6] there is
of course, nothing wrong with
a husband, faced with his wife's initial
refusal to engage in intercourse, in
attempting, in an acceptable way, to
persuade her to change her mind and
that may involve rougher than usual
handling[7] sweetheart, you don't need
a model to work this one out the simple solution
is to prohibit all females
from using these
machines[8]

Zero Sum

It's very unladylike to be yelling in the Parliament[9]
Constant male bashing[10]   It's not
in our values[11]   I'm a country guy so I know[12]

Why would I vote for Malcolm in a skirt?[13]
It's not in our values to push some people down
to lift some people up. That is[14]   how

to fly a plane, ride a horse, and[15]
That is true of gender equality.
We don't want to see women rise

only on the basis of others doing worse.[16]
Men who feel rage as a result of the failure
of their mothers … are highly likely

to project that rage onto future intimate partners,
and often all women.[17]   [I hope he'll get] tough here
with a few backhanders…shove a sock

down her throat[18]   False accusations of violence
being used to destroy men's lives.[19]
Just tell her you know where she lives

and leave it at that. Lol. She will flip[20]
It's not in our values   men having fewer rights[21]
it ain't a good look[22]   We don't want to see women rise

I'm a country guy so I know how to   feel rage
We're sorry. Removing the photo
sent the wrong message[23] about demonising men[24]

Many of the comments …were reprehensible
& we'll work harder to ban trolls
from our pages.[25]   Now that young lady

has a wonderful set of cahoonas[26]
I'm a country guy so I know
how   to project that rage onto future

intimate partners   Lol. She will flip
I've had plenty of mates who've asked me
if they can[27]   project that rage onto ...all women

shove a sock down her throat
and leave it at that. Lol.
We don't want to see women

We're sorry... & we'll work harder
(then you'll no longer be able to attack)[28]
It's very unladylike to yell.

Simmer down

Women have a duty not to provoke men[29]

I'm sensitive to the view of many women
in relation to this but I do think
we shouldn't over-react[30]   If it's just a tap,
like you give your wife when she doesn't have
dinner on the table in time, it doesn't count[31]   Hallelujah,
women cause a lot of problems by nagging, bitching,
and emotionally hurting men. Men cannot bitch back
for hormonal reasons and often have no recourse

but violence[32]   I don't think he was intimidating her,
he was just being persistent. He was being like a little
puppy dog wagging its tail[33]   in accordance with the prevailing
culture of the racing industry[34]   There was nothing
to indicate that the child was an unwilling participant[35]
The man threatened her with a knife, threw her
to the ground and raped her. While deeply shocked
and traumatised, she was not injured[36]   I'm

saying there is as many predator women
as men these days, whereas once upon a
time that may not have been the situation[37].
What male has not occasionally been subject to
the unwanted attentions of a female, even in
trivial matters such as picking imaginary threads from
a jacket lapel[38]   It does happen in the common
experience of those who have been in the law

as long as I have that 'no' often subsequently
means 'yes'[39]   Indulgence is a pleasurable,
curiosity-satisfying activity by an intelligent precocious
girl[40]   It was not a very grave case of rape[41]
at the very bottom of the scale of seriousness[42]   Advocacy
is at its purest form an intellectual exercise where
hormones and chromosomes have no relevance[43]
She admitted owning short skirts
and wearing them socially[44]   There are absolutely as

many predator women, I mean. I've spoken to our guys about it and they tell me[45]

GO AWAY

Go away and stop proving you are a bimbo. You are not fit
to use a computer[46]   Come back when your IQ
is as high as your skirt[47]   I never realised before

how ugly you are[48]   I think what we really need
is more tits[49]   Go away and   wash up[50]
No apology will ever be good enough

for the witch who bathes in male tears[51]   Come back
Women should learn in quietness and full
submission[52]   just let me feel those puppies then[53]

Go away and   just stop shagging men[54]   human females
seem to be outliving their usefulness by 30 or 40 years[55]
Being of the old school, I won't concede

that women are better than men at very much[56]
We know that the best protection for those girls
is that they get themselves into a secure

relationship with a loving husband,
and I want that to happen[57]   Come back
Have your boobs gotten bigger?[58]

There does come a time

Why don't you get a face-lift[59]
There does come a time

when you hang up your swimsuit
because you become a wife or whatever[60]

She is just too old for the times[61]
(the rumours about her are well-known)[62]

It's a shame. She had the chance
to be the tits of the nation, but

she's missed out now[63]   I bet she's now sorry
she burnt her bra all those years ago[64]

She is old and detrimental,[65]   the gallery's
ageing blue heeler[66]   For everything else

there seems to be someone younger, smarter
and yes, prettier; with opinions more worthwhile[67]

We want to freshen up the look[68]

Folly

I really loved the '60s and '70s when life
was so simple and you could slap a woman
on the butt and it was taken as a compliment,

not as sexual harassment[69]   I think it is time for us
alpha males to stand up and refuse
to apologise for our gender[70]   Women are just

an interest group[71]   You have got this bunch
of basically frustrated women who have decided
that if somebody is nude and she is on a poster,

well it's offensive[72]   Men should be trained for war,
women for the recreation of the warrior. All else
is folly.[73]   What do you think you're looking at,

sugar tits?[74]   I will not be harassed by journalists,
even by pretty ones like you. Nick off[75]   I don't
have an adverse attitude to women, except

those who are bitches, including my ex-wife…
When she left me she took all the furniture
except the marriage bed. When I woke up in the morning

the first thought I had was, 'Who's going to get my breakfast?'[76]

I do not permit a woman to teach

Are you familiar with Foucault?[77] Let a woman learn quietly
with all submissiveness. I think It's really great,
professionally, that you don't want to have kids.
You're always so dressed up. Sometimes you come across

as a little abrupt. Can you afford to go on research leave
for a full year? I do not permit a woman to teach
or to exercise authority over a man; rather, she is to remain
quiet. Do you know Rancière? For Adam was formed first,

then Eve; and Adam was not deceived, but the woman was
deceived and became a transgressor. You should read him.
I just don't have time to worry about what I wear. You
come across as sort of masculine, both in your scholarship

and your demeanour. Someone should tell you
to shut up. I like your summer outfit. You're so
energetic all the time. Older women likewise are to be
reverent in behaviour, not slanderers or slaves to much wine.

They are to teach what is good, and so train the young women
to love their husbands and children, to be self-controlled, pure,
working at home, kind, and submissive to their own husbands,
that the word of God may not be reviled. Don't wear yourself out.

I had this amazing professor when I was in college, and he
couldn't have cared less what he looked like. The women
should keep silent in the churches. It was great. For they
are not permitted to speak, but should be in submission,

as the Law also says. You always come across as so cheery.
If there is anything they desire to learn, let them ask
their husbands at home. Of course I consider myself
a feminist. Don't think you're going to take my job.

Solving the problem

Then the Lord God said, 'It is not good
that the man should be alone; I will make him
a helper fit for him.'[78] To the woman he said,

'Your desire shall be for your husband, and he
shall rule over you.' [79] I always thought the orthodoxy was
if you were in a violent relationship you should leave[80]

An excellent wife is the crown of her husband, but
she who brings shame is like rottenness in his bones.[81]
You're obviously a man who the Australian community will,

over the years, get enormous benefit from.[82] This charge
is a lower-end allegation that happens in every second house.[83]
A gracious woman gets honour, and violent men get riches.[84]

Keep calm and slap a bitch.[85] It is better to live
in a desert land than with a quarrelsome and fretful woman.[86]
Using violence against women is a last resort for men,

step three after counselling, buying her chocolates
or taking her out to dinner.[87] Wives, submit to your own
husbands, as to the Lord.[88] Good sex

should be in the gray area between 'tickle fight'
and 'domestic violence'.[89] For man was not made from woman,
but woman from man. Neither was man created for woman,

but woman for man.[90] The patriarchy argument is that men
beat up women in some cases because they hate women.[91]
It is better to live in a corner of the housetop than in a house

shared with a quarrelsome wife.[92] But I don't think
it is about how men look at women, it is about how men
look at themselves. They have lost their self-esteem,

their job, are welfare-dependent, on drugs or alcohol.[93]
These men are just decent citizens.[94]   They use domestic violence
as a coping mechanism to get over all the other crap

they have in their lives. Demonising men and making them
feel worse about themselves is not going to solve
the problem.[95]   A wife's quarrelling
                                            is a continual
                                                      dripping of rain.[96]

Strong Advice

(Barry O'Sullivan v Michael Jackson; descant by Larissa Waters)

How could any living, breathing soul argue against
reconfirmation of the sanctity of life?[97] *She told me
her name was Billie Jean, as she caused a scene.*[98]

My party largely is a conservative party. *She said I am the one,
who will dance   on the floor   in the round.*
You wouldn't have to be a Rhodes Scholar to know

where most of the membership of our party sits
on the issue of abortion. *People always told me
be careful what you do.* Many in the party and outside

would like to lock pregnant women up and bind their arms
and say 'no abortion could occur'. *Don't go around
breaking young girls' hearts.* We as a society in some instances

treat our women just as we did in the 1940s, '50s and '60s,
particularly around pregnancy. *And mother always told me be careful
who you love.* I've spoken to women who wished something like this

had existed when they terminated pregnancies as teenagers.
And be careful what you do, 'cause the lie becomes the truth.
The ladies who have abortions say that it happens

very quickly and they are in an environment with a lot of stress.
Billie Jean is not my lover. A Queensland Liberal-National Party government
must support women and their partners considering abortions

after 18 weeks gestation.[99] *She's just a girl who claims that I am the one.*
We must ensure legislation is enforced requiring women to be
informed of choices when terminating a pregnancy.[100] *But the kid is not my son.*

'Senator O'Sullivan should get his hands and his rosaries
off my ovaries and those of the 10,000 Queensland women
who have an abortion each year, 10,000 women who have the right

to make a decision about their own bodies without the opinion of Senator O'Sullivan getting in the way'.[101]
She says I am the one, but the kid is not my son.

Don Burke's Statement—26 November 2017

I am deeply hurt and outraged at the false and defamatory claims made in your correspondence. It is evident that these baseless claims concern statements from a few ex-employees of CTC productions who bear grudges against me.

I also believe that this publication is opportunistic and intended to severely damage my reputation, by trying to link my alleged behaviour with the appalling behaviour of Harvey Weinstein, which has gained a lot of media traction.

I loathe the reported behaviour of Mr Weinstein and hope that the legal system deals with him in such a way as to prevent this happening again. The bitter irony is that I have had a life-long opposition to sexism and misogyny. Burke's Backyard (BBY) was a lone bastion of anti-misogyny from its inception in 1987. This was evidenced by me deliberately choosing many women to be presenters on this program who were there because they were the very best in their field – truly outstanding women like Densey Clyne, Rosemary Stanton and Jackie French (who was awarded Senior Australian of the year a few years back). These women, in Jackie French's own words, were not the typical media females aged under 30 and with Barbie-Doll figures and Don faced considerable opposition to having them on prime-time TV. They were there because they deserved to be there. The media has never appeared to notice this anti-misogyny.

Even the most cursory of glances at BBY should have evidenced this obvious fact.

For the record, in this matter, I believe I am the classic sitting duck. I created the program BBY. I became co-executive producer of it and was co-director of CTC Productions, the company which made BBY. I am a sitting duck because I was also the main presenter of this eponymously-named program. This is almost unheard of in the television world. I largely ran the program and oversaw the hiring and firing of employees. Inevitably, this led to me being involved in the dismissal of some employees who under-performed or who behaved in an improper manner. Accordingly, there would be a small number of these ex-employees who still bear a strong grudge against me. It is evident, that you obviously been dealing with these ex-employees and as indicated above, you need to do proper screening and background checks in order to publish an accurate record of events.

I absolutely dispute the claims of bullying, and wish to point out that BBY was a prime time TV show where excellence was essential. If even one or two employees in the BBY team were below standard, this could lead to the cancelling of the program and the loss of the jobs of about 40 people. This is the nature of prime time TV. So yes, there was pressure on each and every member of the BBY team to perform at a high level. My perfectionist management was the prime reason for BBY lasting 18 years on prime time TV.

These untrue claims will inevitably destroy my ability to perform my extensive charity work such as my 25-year-plus association with Retina Australia (youth blindness). It will also destroy my association with Asbestos Australia where for over 10 years I have tirelessly worked to save the lives of renovators and tradespeople. I am also associated with charity work of the Psychiatric department of Concord Hospital and many other charities and community groups.

These untrue claims will also destroy my income for the rest of my life. I have solid relationships with Scotts Australia, Celebrity Speakers, and many other groups. Already these mischievous claims have led to some thousands of dollars of cancellations of appearances.

Now, I respond to the specifics of these intentionally destructive claims:

> The rooftop incident never occurred either then nor to any other female ever.
>
> The Alice Springs story never occurred. BBY did not take researchers when filming and I can find no record of this event. No such inappropriate behaviour occurred with anyone and no such video has even been sighted by me. I did not and would not show anything like that to anyone, male or female. No foot pushing or similar episode ever occurred and no comments concerning not working out ever occurred.
>
> My staff and I regarded the CTC Productions workplace as being a very safe workplace and I am very happy to provide female and male witnesses to affirm this.
>
> The story about the reporter quoting me is a total fabrication.
>
> BBY's long term receptionist is a dear friend of mine and no such words were ever uttered by me.

I never commented on the body shape of any **fa**mily membe**r**.

No payouts were ever made, nor were any complaints of this nature ever received by me or anyone in his company. I also was never informed of any complaints or payouts by Channel Nine.

Lastly, it is very evident to me that Ms Spicer has fallen into a small clique of malcontents who were ex-employees of CTC Productions. They must have referred her to others in **this** clique. When Ms Spicer spoke to ex-CTC people who refuted what the malcontents were saying, she appeared to dismiss what they said – it seemed clear that she had made up her mind before contacting them. She had her **"Weinstein" moment** and nothing was getting in its way. This **is unfair and unworthy** journalism. I enclose records of interviews with ex-employees who were contacted by Ms Spicer. All are highly ethical people who **would never tolerate** behaviour such as you have alleged. Jackie French was a reporter on BBY and was Senior Australian of the Year a few years back, Michael Freedman was CEO of BBY for many years as was James O'Sullivan, all three are willing to stand up in public forums or in **court** to verify what they have said. **There are others** in this boat as well.

Don Burke
26 November 2017[102]

Total Fabrication

I am deeply hurt and outraged   This is
almost unheard of in the television world

The rooftop incident   never occurred
either then nor to any other female ever

No such words were ever uttered by me
The Alice Springs story   never occurred

I did not take researchers   when filming
any family member   male or female

I am very happy to pay out female and male witnesses
some thousands of dollars to affirm this.

I largely ran the program and oversaw   the hiring
and firing of employees   Inevitably, this led

to me being involved   in deliberately choosing
many women   to severely damage

For most of the time the main intoxication was
females aged under 30   and with Barbie-Doll figures

excellence was essential   No staff were ever safe
My perfectionist   management   was the prime reason

I have commented on the body shape   of eight publicists
from Channel Nine over the years, 6 were female and 2 were male

The story about the reporter   is not true. The school comment
is not true at all   no such video has even been sighted by me

I regarded any complaints received by me as   total
fabrication   nor would Channel Nine ever tolerate any

No foot pushing or similar episode, no   comments
concerning not working out, no such   inappropriate behaviour

ever occurred   I did not and would not   show anything like that
to anyone   These claims will destroy my ability to perform

my extensive, serious and continuing bullying   This is almost
unheard of in the television world   I am deeply hurt

and outraged   There are others in this boat as well. [103]

Two-hole blues

I sorry I exist, that sucks   You're right, you know:
some days I am a man-looking whore[104]   worthless
bitch   misandrist hag   Other days I'm a humourless

slut   a whining feminazi   a lying SJW cunt   an unfuckable
heifer   a dumb bitch-ass cum-dumpster   Last week
I was definitely a Dworkinite fucktoy   Most days

I am an unrapeable cunt   Guess I'll go get used
for my one and only purpose in this world   gag
on your rod   go learn to shut my damn mouth

get back in the kitchen and drink bleach   Guess I'll go
have my arse split by your cock   Guess I'll be begging
to die tonight at 23:00 hrs   Guess I'll go sit on a chainsaw

& kiss my pussy goodbye   I hope you fuck the gaping hole
I hope the internet will watch   I hope I die of pussy cancer
while my children watch   I hope I kill myself   I hope I get

raped in the mouth   I hope you and your friends will laugh
I hope you're all coming for me   I hope you bang my slut
daughter   I hope you finish off in my eyes

Woke up this morning   expressed an opinion in front of a man
Oh yeah I woke up this morning, had a fully-formed opinion in front of a man
You know the rest, baby   (immediately
          and as hard as he can)

supreme gentleman

Hi , Elliot Rodger[105] . Well , my last video . .
Tomorrow day retribution , day I my revenge humanity
, . last years my life , I puberty , I existence loneliness , rejection
unfulfilled desires , girls me. Girls affection sex love other men , me.
I years old virgin , girl . college , years , , I virgin . torturous .
College time everyone experiences things such sex fun pleasure .
years I rot loneliness , fair .
girls me. I girls I . injustice , crime I , I perfect guy
yourselves obnoxious men , supreme gentleman . I .
[laughs]
day retribution , I sorority house UCSB
I slaughter single spoiled , stuck-up , blond slut I .
girls I much . inferior man I sexual advance , obnoxious brutes .
I great pleasure . , I , truth , superior one , true alpha male .
[laughs]
Yes , I single girl sorority house , I streets Isla Vista slay single person I .
popular kids such lives hedonistic pleasure I rot loneliness years .
look time I , mouse .
Well , I god , animals , animals I slaughter animals .
I god my retribution crime living life me.
popular kids , . Girls , I love , . I girlfriend . I
sex , love , affection , adoration . I unworthy . I crime I . I girls , I .
[laughs]
happy life turn I life , fair . I . Humanity disgusting , wretched ,
depraved species . I my power I nothing single one
mountains skulls rivers blood . I . mercy I none .
[laughs]
my life , I . I long time . I , . girls , , , scum yourselves other men .
men living life , active men . I . I .
 I , annihilation .

only fair

It's an injustice, be a girlfriend. [106]
Tomorrow is the last eight years,
I've had to reduce every single girl.

I'll be annihilated and love to rot in my
revenge against all these years of you.
I'm the true alpha male.

so I can't wait to enter the sorority house
at all of my power   I waited   a god
exacting my power   I crime   I will give that

to come to other men for it   just for it.
and I waited a crime of blood and pleasure.
All those popular kids, never even kissed a god

compared to this. Girls, it's not fair.
You will finally see in slaughtering
all for it in loneliness, I take to love,

it's only fair. Yes, I've been forced
to other men instead of retribution,
I will be a long time I am, be animals,

Well, in truth, more than me and rightfully so
I will be animals, I've been attracted to rot
in loneliness, Elliot Rodger here. [laughs]

You will make you. I hit puberty, depraved
species. I'll be annihilated and love to rot
in my revenge against all these years of you.

and I waited a crime of blood and pleasure.
You will have never get over. You will have
never get over. I'll be annihilated and pleasure

while they throw themselves at these years,
You will have never get over. I will punish you.

Eurydice's Last Sky

(Vindemiatrix) [107]
Her hand
outstretched
—not reaching
for grapes;

. not cradling
a palm-frond
but fending
something,

fending
someone,
Perhaps she
clutched

her keys
like Wolverine,
or Scissor-hands,
knuckle-knifing

the air
around him
Perhaps this
helped

(Auva)
at first,
or perhaps
it merely enraged
him

(Heze)
At 11pm
prone Virgo, high
in the winter
black

(Porrima)
        and pointing
      there, Mars, Pluto,
     Saturn, Jupiter, radar
        dots, glowing,

(Zaniah)
         south to
      northeast, a bright
       trail of crumbs,
        or dripped

(Zavijiava)
         blood,
       leading to
      her other hand,
        the one

(Rijl Al Awwa)
        holding
       her phone,
        sending
       that last

(Syrma)
        useless
     text, 900 metres
      from home
        Take

      responsibility
      for your safety
     said the Super,
       practise

(Spica)
      situational
      awareness.
    Any concerns,
       call
     the police

THE NIGHT BOOK

mothful

you close the door,
leaving your news behind
like a tiny egg
i send my voice after you
it thickens   sweeps soft   from my lips
it has become a dark brown
thing   a furred wing   flailing
i am freighted with
words for you   i carry them
between my teeth   jokes   nicknames   rules for pillow fighting
the particulars of the broken
window   the fact that stage 3 is not
stage 4   how i know about
your shoplifting charge from year 10
& still remember the precise
location of the matchbox car
i hid from you
in 1979   the great results they get from keyhole surgery
these days

the words clog
and swarm
all i am is this
wrong kind of chattering
it makes me think how
after fire certain
blackened saplings
grow their leaves wrong that is all along their arms not out at their fingers
like the charred bark can only
speak its cause over and over having lost
all other habit
but i can't
tell you this or anything
like this
only cough you
the mothdust
from under my tongue

Tree no. 7, Haig Park, Canberra

I'll call you Delvene: a little older, a little rougher,
your hair, your needles, bushy, two-toned   your roots, your sinewy legs
peeking through the worn stonewash   of the ground

Fashion has moved on, by streets, by decades
Your sister Kerry, growing on your sunny side
is getting sick   she hangs on somehow   haggard and spare

So much is dying, something must be being born, Delvene

Whatever you know, you keep it close   Only sometimes you rasp , you sigh
You still worry about lightning   but you're a survivor,
even if these days you find   you have to lift your knees to breathe

Last thoughts at the Shoalhaven

After long walking, stopping
on a wet sandbank, silted
in the elbow of a wide salt river
Shucking shoes, standing

under leaning acacias,
barefoot, silent, feeling
wind's light lift in the hair,
hearing   small chittering

things, fairy wrens   busy
flitting down from thick
branch-lattice *prink   prink
dabblescratch*   seeing them

skip, marking and marking this
stretched wet-sand canvas—
little twig feet, little twig marks
Transfixed, witnessing *chirrup*

hophop   jigglescratch   quick rags
of soft jewel-blue, bark-brown,
their tiny parliament, their jittery
ritual, watching it hiccup closer,

my toes spreading; sinking;
tasting, at their tips, wet silt
Bit by bit, my shadow sweeping
this clock face   this slender, pitted

half-moon beach, feeling them
accept my stillness; shift me
to *safe*: a thing to bliss past
unthinking   Grinning as their frolics

drift to within an inch of my shins
*hophop   jigglescratch   prink   prink
chirrup*   The mingle of tiny high bells
stilling me   bit by bit   Holding a breath

in, I change, willingly: still sinking, slipping
into, becoming   another   thick-ankled
acacia, thinking of wrens, thinking
keep long watch   lean   reach

*roots drink river water
    old leaves   lift in the wind*

Jazz quartet

Wander in, take a wine
        at the little table, red
in the chipped glass, old red
like the lip-stain at the rim, ghost-red
reflected in the sugar bowl, see it spread
like the velvet curtains at the back, got your head
in a fine place, the same place
        where the bass is walking at a walking pace,
under all the ladders, on a roll,
a fat swagger, talking to a talking face
with a soul in a mad blabber, stalking to a spun wheel,
a stagger for the genteel
a plucked line, a strung puppet but it's not mine,
a long spine, a flip to a winning hum
        a drum whisper, a stutter quick
tick of the tipsy clock, a slick
snare skipping softly to an under-slip
carrying a big stick
a brush hushing to a finger click,
sleight of hands in a summer trick
        piano in a hurry, coming down
scurry bumble on the slung stairs, the old brown
the dirty rum, pass the muddled jugs round
to the huddled scrum, hit the floor
the sure switch, the doors twitch, start the running
with the rising cup, coming up, stalk and spin
with the crystal napkin rings, swing a grin as you slither in
to the idea   of a chandelier   the brittle glitter,
        the sweet shine, the sax pouring honey wet
down the bannisters, the swoop and spread,
the wide howl and the dog's dead, the big bed
with the feathers and the foghorns, where you let
loose balloons in the wide sky, let
the white tiger out, and he stops by,
        mute as the new sun
coming up, the shop's shut
game's up, done and dusted like the long night
the lost fight, the wrong light shining in your strong wine
pleads you to leave it for a long time

'til tomorrow will be just fine
        'til tomorrow will be just fine

Bloodnut Gut-wrench

In the front window of Salty Joe's, a red-haired
man is sipping tomato juice, scanning the horizon, eyes
on the scarred grey sea   snarling into his phone
I told you, I have a couple of days
at the most   I avoid his ice eyes, shuddering
at his orangutan head, at the hair on his
forearms, a matted almost-pelt of fishing wire, gone
burred and sandy   They are mutants, you know   All
the red-haired blue-eyed people descend from the same game-changer,
the same alien   A man can be a man
and yet apart, an animal, mottled, exotic, a giraffe
sitting in the front window of Salty Joe's, wearing
the face of the Vikings, the Normans   His snarl
is the sound of a sweaty melee, beaching, leaping
a keel   Only melanomas can kill them   No home
but the restless salty sea   I know in my
bones they are bad   (am relieved my own auburn
has silvered to frost, my own freckles have paled
on my hull   that the fire-haired changeling I carried
is silent   is drowned) and I know in my
bones   that the raiding is starting again   He sips
juice   The corners of his mouth run with dark
tomato   *Yeah let's get on it*   told you   Bloody
boat people   inexorable   our axes will sing again   soon

Deru Kui

出る杭は打たれる *('Deru kui wa utareru')*:
'The stake that sticks up will be hammered down'
—*Japanese proverb*

Don't expect to last long, or like lasting. Savour, instead, this
enormity, this arena of baying hundreds, into which you protrude,
rudely, perpendicularly. Marvel at the typhoon of outrage,
utter and visceral, gathering promptly at the pinpoint insult of you.
Know now that nothing you ever said can be
unsaid, but also that none of it matters.
It is only your angle they care about, your insouciant, bare-faced
whole ninety degrees of self-possession. You
are their nightmare, their mere anarchy, and they cannot stand it.
Untie your shoes, remove your jacket, show them your empty pockets—
they stampede regardless. Know also this frenzy is crucial, it reveals
all that is hidden, unquestioned, maps it like radioactive dye,
renders it visible, gives it co-ordinates. That is your value,
even as your own sky falls, keeps falling as a series of circular metal stamps,
ringing, ringing, rendering you, once again
unremarkable, ringing, ringing, ringing you down.

Michael Collins

'Not since Adam has any human known such solitude as Mike Collins is experiencing during this 47 minutes of each lunar revolution when he's behind the Moon with no one to talk to except his tape recorder aboard Columbia.'
—Mission Control, Apollo 11 Mission Log, July 21, 1969, 9.44am

Not-landing, too. Not-landing. Somebody had to.
I liked it. Not-landing. For twenty-seven hours. I

loved it. The far side, especially. Everyone I had ever known,
every city, field, tussock, insect. Wiped. Unreachable

behind that great bleached wall. Me, falling past it, in radio silence,
three-quarters of an hour at a time. It changed me.

Not landing, not wanting to land. (The lunar dust
came in with them, anyway, smelling of cordite). They

descended, stamped their stark footprints in, planted
their flag, their cameras. I floated, steering their only lifeboat.

They lugged and wrangled; positioned the solar-wind sail,
the seismograph, the laser reflector. I flowered, witnessing

the humanless infinite, leaving, returning, leaving again, returning.
They ascended, strewing their hammers, their chisels, abandoning

their lonely boots; that plaque. I waited, suspended, exulting,
the craters scrolling, black, white, black, white, grey.

Julia after Tony's boning

14 September 2015

...
and
who's to say
she did not, that night
make, in effigy, his head—
an onion, perhaps, split; spread to
wingnut—and who's to say she did not
take up, with relish, a pair of Tim's scissors
and stab and stab, rending the membranes
(those sheer lady-veils), releasing the stinging
pungence of witch-rage, wreaking that
sharp, sweet havoc :
Fulvia's hairpin
in Cicero's
tongue

Ba by Joy

(In an alternate universe, Barnaby Joyce apologises for the 2017 Same-Sex Marriage Plebiscite)

Guys, are you **Ready? This** is **the truth.** I peddled the bitterest political just lie legal rights how deeply hurt how deeply hurt them. how deeply dragged my people how deeply this personal issue—deeply personal issue— into the public arena. I am a shadow now. But I think this is vitally important how we differentiate between the public and the private. Thank you.

**Ba by Joy ,
13 February 2018**

DIY Empire

Trust is getting more expensive. I know
how those people in the Weimar newsreels felt
(except that I don't) but I kid myself I can empathise—

How barrows-ful of cash were required, and yet
insufficient
Never bring a screwdriver to a drill fight, you will only
go down, under-spun, orphaned by light
Every moment so irrevocable, a nail in a nail-gun, and yet

we live our whole lives pretending otherwise,
extenuating

At the going down of the sun, the cashbox must be reconciled   the greasy coins
laid out   we are short   there are dozens of zinc-ed
lips insisting, they will not be silenced, and so I

heave myself into the promotional wheelbarrow, naked but for cheesecloth
artistically arranged   I am moon-like and perfectly bruised, but with
no means of locomotion—perhaps I am hoping to be
grabbed like a dangling handbag, possessed as recompense

for all the unsecured debts, the collapse of this
Rome, everything taken and sullied—OK perhaps just as the first instalment,
one of billions, just enough to cover one tree, one creek, one family
man-handled

22 November 2018

Go therefore and make disciples of all nations.
Clouds hang over North Sentinel Island.
A man takes a selfie on a boat with another man

leaning on the rail behind him.   John Allen Chau on a boat.
How are they to believe in Him of whom
they have never heard?   In the wake of the 2004 tsunami

this member of the Sentinelese tribe was photographed
firing arrows at a helicopter.   *And how are they to hear*
without someone preaching?   The US missionary

wanted to live with the tribe on the remote island.   *For necessity*
is laid upon me   Tribespeople killed two Indian fishermen
in 2006 when their boat broke loose and drifted

onto the shore.   *Woe to me if I do not preach the gospel!*
Mr Chau offered gifts to the tribesmen, such as a football and fish.
And this gospel of the kingdom will be proclaimed

throughout the whole world as a testimony to all nations,
and then the end will come
                              American missionary killed

by protected tribe was a passionate adventurer and Christian.
The family of John Allen Chau have asked that no-one
be punished for his death.   Sentinelese scare off rescuers

trying to remove John Allen Chau's body.   Clouds hang
over North Sentinel Island.   A dark figure,
photographed from high above, pointing a bow upwards.

FUGAL STATES

Fugal state

Always returning upon the paths of time,
we are neither ahead nor behind; late is early,
near is far
Maurice Blanchot, The Writing of the Disaster

You are always beginning again—
it is only a matter of degree:
you walk into a room, forgetting

the book you came looking for, walk out
with a dirty glass   you lay down
another ring   without realising

like a tree   it doesn't hurt a bit
You are always beginning again:
you walk into the forest, forgetting,

there is a storm, there is a morning,
you walk out, trailing possibilities
from your hands   they drip, like

snapped branches   There was a storm,
there was a morning   There was
a name, once, a specific and grievous

history, a mobile number, a particular sequence
of houses, an immunity to certain indignities,
there was more and more forgetting

Entering a room full of bonsai, you breathe
moss, and cypress, and the clean, bald smell
of long-dry river-stones   The air hums

with age, with what the trees have known
and have forgotten   and will know again
they are always beginning

you breathe, you dream   you have been
reborn   as a small ceramic deer
You sit under the *momiji*, the scarlet

baby's hands of the Japanese maple,
in a forest small enough
to fit on a dinner plate
and begin
again

Apes rule

Use pearl—
pale, sure
   pearl. Use
purse. Ale.

Leer up as
re-use pal;
re-use lap.

Pure sale.

*Pa, reel us,
repeal us,
repel us*: a
user plea.

A repulse.

Pale ruse,
pleasure.

Lures ape;
rules ape.

red, white and window

The April air above the office blocks is guileless blue
but too warm to trust. On the corner there is a situation, cordoned off,
    a jumble

of witches' hats and high-vis. The building says *nab*. The logo
    is a bloodied red star. One point
is striped with absences, sharp parallel scars, twin zebra-marks
    of gouge, they gesture

to the window washer, white helmeted, in his slowly rising cage,
    who tends to the dust. He bathes
the glass which is keeping the air out, the workers in. He thinks *nab*
    means opportune theft
Inside, on the window ledge, a dusty white peace lily calls
    to the white helmet. Beside it a woman

with a headset and bitten nails, her roots starting to show. Her screen
    says *nab*. She tends to it
like a duty, like dusty window, it does not always obey, there are
    wilful red absences

starting to show. In her mind, a dream of a day with no gouges, no
    glass, a portal she sails through,
opportunely, on a Vespa, in a sundress, past all the situations,
    unmarked again, impossible to catch.

in/sight

'Interior departures (17): Tracy', gelatin silver photograph 18.8 x 18.6 cm image; 23.5 x 20.9 cm sheet, by Ann Balla, 1980.

I see you, looking. You are breathing, a little
heavily. I see you, gazing, at the pooled shadow
in her collarbone; at her armpit, its intimate tuft.

You are licking your lips. You want to pluck her
like a flower, like the idea of a flower. Her slender
bicep, her serious mouth. She is practising her freestyle,

trying her power, trying her goggles on for size.
She will need them, to see through, under water.
Dangling above her, the glistening certainty

of what this is, what you think you are owed.
A black swallow, stiff-winged, inverted, inert.
You want to pluck her; vase her in glass crenellations;

trap most of her under water, til she sags and wilts,
til she blows. I watch you, watching her. I keep
watch. The room ghosts around me,

around the both of me, we are misting
and partially see-through. We make our own frame
with our elbows, our bones. We will ourselves solid,

angular, unpluckable, unplucked. I see through
the room, the frame, the place where the both of us
merge. She sees through the world under water. I see
                                         through you.

like anything

the casuarinas stirring   the storm wind   four brown chimneys guarding Sydney Park
tilt, shake, look again
Sydney is stirring your guarded park
       casuarinas in the four brown winds
              chimneys of storm

anything at all, anything you like,
each time a little twist, a warp

public library   strip lighting   patterned concrete   violent neon print
a little like anything:
neon library
       printed concrete light
              patterns of violence
                    public stripping

change all time, each slight, anything likes it

coloured glass chips
tumbled in a mirror-pipe
the shifts, mesmerising
and possibly significant

anything at all, anything you like
      is like you again, and never,
           and again like you, and again never, and never again

today's tickly throat   last night's year 6 homework   plastic bottles, blu-tac

tic-tac-plastic-homework
      today's blue night
           6 years of bottles
                his last throat

Some assembly required

You feel you are being followed   Perhaps it is only the wires
out the window of the train They are tracing your suspended

journey in liquorice parallels travelling and travelling hovering
in an infinite deferral of touch Perhaps you are pretending

it is Sunday, sprawling over a seat and a seat and a seat all lax,
all lone and fluid Perhaps you resent the man who shuffles on

at Milson's Point   who lowers and sighs to sit   right thigh
jammed against yours   At the same time perhaps you realise

this was always going to happen it has only been a matter of time
You may struggle to accept the gift of his odour, his aura

of urine and cigarette his breath like lighter fluid You note he is
wearing work clothes   and some kind of lanyard You may be tremored,

slightly, by the jiggling of his right thigh   He is Morse-coding
someone steadily, intently jiggling and jiggling He sings himself,

softly, *helme helme melme flo flo helme gelme* You are intent
on the window   on the wires   on the never-ending oblong of their

refusal to meet   *helme helme melme flo flo helme gelme oww*
Perhaps if you looked at him now   you would see flames

pour from his mouth, feel the shock of his words carbonising
between his teeth   *helme helme helpme getme ouu* Beyond the wires

you are watching a structure approach   somewhere near Artarmon
with every jiggle   the pieces assemble themselves   into a beacon

some kind of communications   tower   *helme helpme getme flo
flo helme gelme out* The thing is an elegant   bricolage   a model

with the joins inked in   Perhaps you did not notice the baby
get on at Wollstonecraft   but it is incontrovertibly here, now

redly refusing to breastfeed   wailing   *Helme helpme melme flo
flo helme getme ouuu*   You are still watching the structure approach

the baby is an elegant   bricolage   its cries are carbonising   somewhere
between Milson's Point and Artarmon   it would eat   the liquorice

parallels   if it could   it wants the wires   to cross   Perhaps you look down
to realise   you also are wearing work clothes   and some kind of lanyard

and by now   you fully comprehend   the structure   You sing yourself,
softly *helme helpme gelme flo flo helme getme out*   Perhaps you realise

it is time   it has always been time   for you   to get to work

Marks

(or, Lt Wm Bligh notes the distinguishing features of the *Bounty* mutineers)

It is given to so few of us,
this clarity

Fletcher Christian aged 24 years 5'9" High	
Complexion	Dark, & very swarthy
Hair	Blackish or very dark brown
Make	Strong
Marks	Star tattooed on the left breast and on the backside. His knees stands a little out and may be called a little bow-legged

(They have left him his pen
He is making a kind of ledger,
scratching at the bitter pages

as if these columns
will ever balance)

George Stewart Aged 23 years 5'7" High	
..	...
has the	small face and black eyes

of all your bad luck
scurrying straight at you, a rat
across a mooring-rope

(He will make proper account, for there will be a reckoning
Adrift though he is, he will tally the blackguards
like stolen cargo, like the lost breadfruit seedlings
—months and months of His Majesty's work
thrown into the sea)

	Peter Haywood Aged 17, 5' 7"
..	...
and	*well-proportioned*
	had not done growing

—as if such a wound, such a theft, is ever done growing—

his	*Manx accent*

will convict him, apparently— that and

his	*three-legged tattoo*

The Pacific has blotted the ink, we will never know whether

	Edward Young Aged 22, stood 5'1" or 5'7"
but he remains	*Dark* of complexion,
	Strong of make,
...	...
has	*Rather a bad look,*
has	*lost several of his foreteeth and those that remain are all rotten*

This clarity
given to so few
This certainty
that what was lost
was lost on this day
at this hour
at the hands of a man

with	*a small mole on the left side of the throat*

Did the Chiefs of O-Taheite
keep their own
ledger of thieves
dealers in bad faith
liars

Did they note somewhere
each particular indignity
so many women kidnapped
so many houses burned, so many canoes
so many balances of power
left holed, left listing

The grandmothers must have
surely
inside their implacable heads

—the litany of wounds, of thefts, is never done growing

They have always known
when someone commandeers
your only vessel
sails it clean away

the recital
of each imperfection
may be all the lifeboat
that is left to you

how it can then become
a matter of utmost importance
that the perpetrator

is	*subject to violent perspiration and particularly in his hands so that he soils any thing he handles*

Newcastle reckoning

The Moreton Bay fig trees have received the signal
They are dropping their sticky treasure-bags,
the small coins of seed spill and scatter in dark clumps
I am sitting in a house on a hill, *The Hill*, sitting
in a pale green chair, high up

in the hot blue air above the estuary, sitting
and being filmed, it is the first time
I have ever been on camera
and known it, the shock and squirm
seeing my own jaw obscenely working, my own

smug cheeks below my vacant eyes
We are filming in a house on a hill, The Hill,
but I do not know its Awabakal name
and I have neither sought nor received
permission to enter here

I am rude and unprotected, jaw working
and working, sitting like a pale green insult
The birds in the fig trees are raucous, they keep
ruining the recording, we have to do take after take
There is an angry man mounting the stairs

from the basement, he is making noises with his mouth
about insurance and preconditions   We do not
comprehend him but it seems we must leave
The smell from the basement is cold
off the convict-hewn sandstone, it is

clammy and cemetery, rotten with loss
We pack up the camera, move on It is a stifling
afternoon, the breeze keeps failing, my breath
is shallow and I am slick behind the knees
The fallen figs stick to my shoes,

they are trying to tell me something
about preconditions, about the reproductive
cycle of betrayal   As the dusk comes in
I am sleeved with mosquitoes
I want to tell them to leave, but I do not know

their Awabakal names   The half-moon rises,
magnified in the hot air, it knows
I have neither sought nor received permission,
it knows about my people, it has watched them
as they slit the skin of the land upriver, has watched them,

working and working, obscenely
gouging the coal from under her ribs
The birds cry and cry again in the fig-branches,
they are making noises with their bird-mouths
trying to tell me something

about treasure, and small coins, and sandstone;
about memory, shallow and slick   We stop and sit on the steps
halfway down to King St   The old broken-in-half moon,
a headstone, inverted, showing her bone-self, hangs
clammy and cemetery over the asphalt, over Civic Park

over all the unmarked graves   There is an anger
mounting from under the fig-roots, magnified
by each insult   We do not comprehend   It wants us to leave
This air is rotten with loss, but we are still sitting,
and sitting, living on it, breathing it in

VENTRILOQUIES

Two poems by Sulpicia

V: From my sick bed

Sulpicia 5 (Tibullus 3, 17)
Cerinthus, will you keep faith with your girl
now fever's struck this tired body down?
I can't beat back this dismal thing unless
you too want me to fight it, and to win.
If you can watch me suffer, and stay calm,
what is the point in getting up again?

VI: Remorse at my lack of candour

Sulpicia 6 (Tibullus 3, 18)
Last week we stoked each other up so high
you saw me incandescent—yet, last night,
afraid to show you I was still on fire
I went and left you all alone, my light.
Of all the clueless things I've ever done,
may I regret this most—or lose this flame.

Pairs

By Mizuki Misumi

My shoes:
For rainy days and snow days,
these black ones, warm and lightweight
For fine days, kind-of-special days,
these pretty leather ones, bright green like new shoots

His shoes:
For rainy days and snow days,
those strong ones, that look like
       you could climb a mountain in them
For normal, fine days,
those brown leather ones, the colour of spring soil

When we come in to the entryway
there they are on the left,
lined up ready on the beige tiles

This is me, who famously can't survive
on just one pair of shoes
but for now
as long as there are these two pairs,
       and those two pairs
it is enough

Map of the peninsula

By Harumi Kawaguchi

The path I walked in summer follows the sea
—at night, alone, I trace it with my finger
This autumn paper is pleasantly cool, smooth,
dried out
Just there, at the tip of the peninsula, where I couldn't
        go any further,
where I stopped still and looked up, beneath the sky
—that wetness which welled up, spilled over,
where on earth did it dry up to?
They say the waves have been at the lone offshore island,
        wearing it away;
that day, it was glinting there in the open sea
but on this map it is nowhere to be found

'Wet Island'

My lips, pronouncing the unrecorded name
quiver slightly as they open, and so
my finger leaves the paper
and plucks a single grape from the bunch
        on the autumn table
Sealed inside,
the sweet wet young juice has deepened
I bring it to my lips, I make it feel like summer's mouth
        is on mine
it pulls the glimmer of night along with it and drips,
trickling along my arm—my peninsula—
and dropping onto on the cooled map
records my fever with a small round mark

Welcome Home

By Harumi Kawaguchi

Happy Birthday! He came home with a box, more than an armful,
       and held it out to me, grinning.
Instinctively taking it from him and staggering a little at the
       unexpected weight
I messed up the timing of saying Thank you but this was because my
       birthday was over nine months away
—and since there is no question that this man who has been living
       with me for years would mistake the date,
I thought perhaps, just for a moment, that I myself
       was misremembering it
but that is, of course, unlikely   <*grin*>
I tear open the wrapping paper with gusto, and a glass aquarium
appears   is born
But it is empty
We don't own any beautiful tropical fish, cute turtles, gorgeous
       chameleons. I don't know what to do with it
To start with... I try putting it on top of the TV unit, where
       our television that stopped working used to be. It goes there
       unexpectedly well.
Perhaps they are the same kind of thing
In saying that   that time the two of us carried the long-ago broken
       TV in our arms to the large waste drop-off
to throw it away, we looked back at it again and again, as if we had
       abandoned a *child* in the woods,
and we ran, the two of us. The blue of the dawn sky lit up my skin
       like a broken screen and I felt as if the colour
       would never come off
He has changed out of his work clothes, and opens a can of beer
       on the sofa in front of the TV unit
It might be nice to sit next to him and stare together at the empty
       aquarium, but since this is a special occasion
I decide to try getting inside it
Straddling with my right leg, guiding my left leg in...   what was it
       made that faint creaking sound? The aquarium?
       The TV unit? Me?

When I hug my knees and make myself round, I fill it out just right
I'm so happy. This is just what I wanted. Who said that? Me?
        The TV unit? The aquarium?
The glass panels kiss the skin of my arms and the soles of my feet,
    like cool fresh water
It is unexpectedly good
He is smiling, drinking his beer, looking at the aquarium
    with the same face he used to watch the TV with.
    Nothing in his head.
I changed into my pyjamas, and climbed in again without really
    thinking. I was so comfortable like that I fell fast asleep.
    And so
as if it were the natural course of things, from the next day on
    it became my nest
Every time I come back after going out I say 'I'm home' toss my
    bag aside take off my clothes discard them say Goodnight
    and climb
inside it
<squeak>
He comes home, quietly seats himself on the sofa,
    and draining the can of beer he has opened, gazes
at me, sleeping
at the empty aquarium
or the blank screen of the no-longer-there broken television
head full of nothing
I'm home goodnight *welcome home* I'm home welcome home
    goodnight welcome home *welcome home*
Something is being born
I am full of nothing
When I get broken this time he'll be on his own, perhaps
    he'll need a trolley, for the day he'll have to take me
    to the large waste drop-off
I'd better give him a trolley for a birthday present.
    Happy Birthday!
I'm home My skin is the blue colour of dawn

Sweet nothing

By Harumi Kawaguchi

This feeling, that I have something to say to someone,
quivers underneath the dark night
It is as if I have thin, translucent wings
coiled about me, wetly
protruding from my back at half length,
and I can't even lie down to sleep
I don't have a special 'someone'
I have absolutely nothing special to say
Even so, in the cold darkness I open my eyes wide
Maybe I could even say
I LOVE YOU
even *that*, just to have said *something*.
My lips, like two petals on a rain-soaked flower,
like my wings,
press wetly together, then dry out and part, unfolding
I'm trying to shape the ghost of the unsaid words
        with my mouth
but it's like pretending to beat my wings—even if I do it,
I can't get anywhere
Outside this body, everywhere is the boundless world
Is it the world that is cold and sweet?
Or is it me, this body that touches it?
In the morning it will come at me from over there,
a new light, arriving as a monster
I will open out my painful wings, and flap them
This tiny insect I seem to have become
will melt away any minute, no doubt,
like a candy on a tongue
Against this light we call 'today'
I'll etch the shape of this body, its darkness
Go on, fly

21 buttons for Yoshiko 包み釦二十一個

A poem on the wedding dress of Yoshiko Creagh (nee Ishikawa), made in Tokyo, 1956, held in the National Museum of Australia.

1 一個目 *ikkome*
If you cannot procure buttons in the correct colour,
you can cover them in fabric.
The pleats in the skirt are impeccable, precise.
A pale cloud of tulle swells underneath.
There are twenty-one hand-covered buttons,
tiny silver-shelled creatures, studding
each wrist, trailing down the front of the bodice.

2 二個目 *ni-kome*
Even the simplest,
cheapest buttons can look truly elegant
when covered correctly.
She wasn't sewing when she met him.
There was more money
waiting tables
at the Base cafeteria.
Every day, the pink, loud men,
jostling, chewing
with their pink, loud mouths.

3 三個目 *san-kome*
Take a circle of fabric, not too large:
when you draw the edges together
over your button, they should not quite
meet in the middle.
The sour smell of Western food.
She noticed how *he* ate –
with his mouth closed. His hair:
how it curled and waved,
every which-way, how he looked
innocent, earnest, kind,
a little unruly.

4 四個目 *yon-kome*
Too much fabric
will bunch up
and become unwieldy.
They say there are hundreds
like her. War Brides. 戦争花嫁.
To her it sounds
like they're married to War,
like War is a husband
with hundreds of wives.

5 五個目 *go-kome*
If your button has some kind of texture
you would like to hide, use a piece of felt
the same size as the top of your button.
Sometimes War is called
Clem, or Harry, and lives
in Toowoomba, or Mount Isa.
Her own War is Victor
from Brisbane, with the unruly hair.
When he asks, she enlists
without hesitation
and starts sewing again
in earnest.

6 六個目 *rokkome*
Knot your thread and work
from the wrong side
of the fabric.
The day comes: she is clad
in the silver brocade,
the bodice is tight, tight,
but the buttons hold
and look marvellous.
Even in her kitten heels,
the top of her head only reaches
to Victor's lower lip.

7 七個目 *nana-kome*
Start weaving your needle in and out
of the edge of your circle,
all the way around. The smaller your weave,
the better the outcome.
The tulle swishes against her thighs.
They thrash through it, dolphins in a net.
Her pearl necklace, just peeping
through the deep V at her throat.
On the outside of her lacy glove,
the gold ring, glinting.

8 八個目 *hakkome*
To finish, place your button
back in the centre of your circle,
then pull your thread. It will cinch
right around the button,
creating a nice cover for it.
Four months later
she is sitting on the deck
of the steamship *Tai Yuan*
She kept the picture:
four girls together,
all of them married to War now.
Demure skirts, slender-waisted cardigans,
pale dainty shoes, crossing that
unknowable sea. Wondering.

9 九個目 *kyuu-kome*
To secure, knot the thread-end,
keeping the cinched in fabric
nice and tight.
Brisbane. *Bu-ri-zu-bē-ng.* Strange flowers
with their pink and yellow tongues.
The muddy smell of the river,
those stilted houses.
Nowhere to buy soy sauce
or *tōfu*, or seaweed.
No one has even heard of *miso*.

10   十個目   *juu-kome*
People refusing to serve her
in the dusty shops.
Go back to Japan! She can't,
of course, not ever, now, she is
a shameful thing, *sensō hanayome* 戦争花嫁,
War Bride. The neighbourhood
would be whispering, endlessly.
Fallen woman. Prostitute.
Sensō hanayome. Traitor.
(When you draw the edges together,
they will not quite meet in the middle)

11   十一個目   *juu-ikkome*
Victor told her
about the *Immigration Restriction Act*,
how it meant, Only Whites Allowed.
How the Minister said once,
"[I]t would be the grossest act
of public indecency to permit a Japanese
of either sex to pollute Australia."
(If you cannot procure buttons in the correct
colour, you can cover them in fabric.
Knot your thread and work
from the wrong side)

12   十二個目   *juu-ni-kome*
They had to change the rules
for the War Brides, slowly,
grudgingly. Poor Cherry Parker,
Sakuramoto-san: four years,
two children, all in limbo, waiting.
(In and out, in and out.
Always from the wrong side)

13   十三個目   *juu-san-kome*
The air in Brisbane, sticky,
like a Tokyo summer,
but all the time. Palm trees,
green and waving, even in the city.
On the side of a tram: ARNOTT'S SAO.

She had to ask what it meant.
(Pull your thread. Knot the end,
keeping the cinched in fabric
nice and tight)

14 十四個目 *juu-yon-kome*
The Army gave classes. She tried
to pay attention. Giggling behind her hand
in Japanese with the other girls.
Pay attention. Teach your children
English only. Give them
English names.
(Nice and tight.
The smaller your weave,
the better the outcome)

15 十五個目 *juu-go-kome*
Seven years on, she's NATURALISED
(na-chu-ra-rai-zu-du)
The Queen is on the piece of paper,
radiant in yellow taffeta,
in diamonds. Such power,
to divide the natural
from the unnatural
with only a word.
(Your button has some kind of
texture you would like to hide)

16 十六個目 *juu-rokkome*
The typewritten details
on the Certificate
so awkwardly placed
on the dotted lines, so ugly:
eleventh of June nineteen sixtythree
Back home it would be calligraphy,
and it would be impeccable.
(Even the simplest,
cheapest buttons
can look truly elegant
when covered correctly)

17 十七個目 *juu-nana-kome*
With Victor, it was fine.
She was still married to War, in a way:
always moving, base after base.
It was fine. Fine. The children came.
Singapore, Korea, Australia again.
Fine, fine. Until it wasn't.
(To finish, place your button
back in the centre of your circle,
then pull your thread)

18 十八個目 *juu-hakkome*
She stays in Australia,
even after the divorce.
She has friends, her children,
a life. Independence of a kind.
Besides, what the Queen gives,
the Emperor takes away:
the law says, she cannot be Japanese
any more.
(Too much fabric
will become unwieldy)

19 十九個目 *juu-kyuu-kome*
She starts sewing again.
Kimono this time.
So different to Western dresses,
but no less precise.
(Start weaving your needle in and out)

20 二十個目 *ni-juu-kome*
With *kimono*
you must pay attention
to both the inside
and the outside, the way
the fabric folds and turns over.
(Knot your thread and work)

21 二十一個目 *ni-juu-ikkome*
With *kimono*
the inner and the outer
are always showing,
there is never
a 'wrong side'.
(And no buttons, of course.
No buttons at all.)

Afterword

This book is a strange and possibly lopsided assemblage, not unlike its cover image. Its central concern is gendered violence, both verbal and physical. These poems also extend their gaze to violences perpetrated in the names of colonialism, nationalism and capitalism. It has been called my angriest book yet. Despite this, there are also poems celebrating moments of connection and wonder.

The text includes an earlier found-text chapbook, *Listen, bitch*, plus new work from the last three years. The 'Listen, bitch' poems are an exercise in listening very closely to what powerful men say, in public, about women. By taking careful note of the snarlings of what Kate Manne calls 'the law enforcement branch' of the current patriarchal order[1], these poems attempt to map the lines women are still not supposed to cross in contemporary Australia, and to document the consequences suffered when they do. The work is (broadly) ranged along a continuum of violence: the further you go into the section, the more brutal and physical are the costs borne by the women in the poems. This work was enabled and inspired by the now-25-year-old Ernie Awards for Sexist Behaviour (for more, see http://ernies.com.au/ and Meredith Burgmann and Yvette Andrews' *The Ernies Book: 1000 Terrible Things Australian Men Have Said About Women)*. Many thanks to Meredith and Yvette for permission to build on their work in this way.

'The space inside his fist' section is intended as a companion to the 'Listen, bitch' section, asking broader questions about masculinity, its performance and its consequences.

The other parts of the book address a range of public and private concerns, ranging from state-sanctioned theft to the way memory works (or doesn't). They include dreamscapes and imagined histories, personal lyrics, sonic and structural experiments, ekphrastic pieces and translations from Japanese and Latin.

I hope, amongst all that, you can find something to enjoy, or argue with, or both.

July 2020

---

1   Kate Manne, "The Logic of Misogyny", *Boston Review*, July 11 2016

Notes

THE SPACE INSIDE HIS FIST

Orion as a woman unhelped by White Ribbon is based on the constellation of Orion as seen from the southern hemisphere during our summer (with the red giant Betelgeuse in the lower right). Each stanza of the poem corresponds to a star in the constellation. The events in the poem are based on a real news story from the UK but have been transposed to this hemisphere and fictionalised. This poem was exhibited as an artwork (with the stanzas placed in their constellation positions on the body of a black dress) in the Belconnen Arts Centre exhibition 'Postcards from the Sky', Feb 8-Mar 17, 2019.

LISTEN, BITCH

The poems in this section are mostly found-text assemblages. A significant number are composed wholly or partly of public statements nominated for Ernie Awards for Sexist Behaviour (http://ernies.com.au/) in their respective years. See *The Ernies Book: 1000 Terrible Things Australian Men Have Said About Women* (Meredith Burgmann and Yvette Andrews, Allen & Unwin, 2007). Many thanks to Meredith and Yvette for permission to use their corpus of Ernie nominees in this way.

Ernie Ecob as a Bare-Bellied Joe

1   Ernie Ecob is the man for whom the 'Ernie Awards' for Sexist Behaviour are named. He famously made the remark 'women only want to be shearers for the sex' during his time as Secretary of the Australian Workers' Union (the old Shearers' Union). See Burgmann and Andrews, *op. cit.*

Sweetheart,

2   John Dawkins, Federal Treasurer, to Liberal MP Kathy Sullivan, 1994.
3   Sheikh Taj el-Dene Elhilaly, Mufti (speaking about rape victims), 2007.
4   Tim Fischer, Deputy Prime Minister, 1998.
5   Martin Ferguson, ACTU President (referring to women unionists campaigning for paid maternity leave), 1995.
6   Iain MacLean, WA Liberal MP, 1998.
7   Justice Derek Bollen, SA Supreme Court, 1994.
8   Rev. Fred Nile, NSW Christian Democrat MP, on how to solve the Big Dipper roller coaster noise problem at Sydney's Luna Park ('Engineers have said the high pitched screams of females are breaking the noise levels'), 2006.

Zero Sum

9   Sue Hickey, Speaker of the Tasmanian House of Assembly (LIB), admonishing Deputy Opposition leader Michelle O'Byrne (LAB) for interjecting during debate, 31 July 2019 https://www.abc.net.au/news/2019-07-31/tasmania-speaker-unladylike-comment-blasted-in-parliament/11370914.
10 Media commentator and sex therapist Bettina Arndt, 2019. Full quote: 'Feminism...It's all about rules and regulations to advantage women at the expense of men. Constant male bashing. False accusations of violence being used to destroy men's lives. Women denying men access to their children. There are endless rules in our society now which are about demonising men'. Winner, The Elaine Award (for remarks least helpful to the Sisterhood), Ernie Awards, 2019.

11 Scott Morrison Prime Minister of Australia, International Women's Day, 2019. Full quote: 'It's not in our values to push some people down to lift some people up. That is true of gender equality. We don't want to see women rise only on the basis of others doing worse'.
12 Family man, Nationals MP Andrew Broad, writing to a Sugar Baby website, 2019. Full quote: 'I'm a country guy so I know how to fly a plane, ride a horse and f**k my woman'.
13 Tony Abbott (reportedly) to Julie Bishop when she rang him for support in the Liberal Party leadership contest in August 2018 (Peter Hartcher in the *Sydney Morning Herald*, March 30, 2019 https://www.smh.com.au/politics/federal/how-the-liberals-got-stuck-in-a-long-demented-cycle-of-vengeance-20190326-p517sz.html).
14 Scott Morrison, International Women's Day, 2019.
15 More from Nationals MP Andrew Broad on the Sugar Baby website. See note above.
16 Scott Morrison, International Women's Day, 2019.
17 Author John Marsden. Winner, Celebrity Silver Ernie, 2019.
18 Alan Jones, 2GB Broadcaster, about NZ Prime Minister Jacinda Ardern., 2019. Full quote: '[I hope Prime Minister Scott Morrison will get] tough here with a few backhanders.. She's a clown, Jacinda Ardern... I just wonder whether Scott Morrison is going to be fully briefed to shove a sock down her throat'.
19 Bettina Arndt, 2019. See note above.
20 Police Officer Neil Punchard, texting a woman's details to her violent former husband, 2019 (https://www.theguardian.com/australia-news/2019/mar/27/queensland-police-breached-privacy-of-domestic-violence-victim-by-leaking-her-details).
21 John Setka, CFMEU Secretary, to the CFMEU executive, 2019. Full quote: 'The work of Rosie Batty has led to men having fewer rights'.
22 Coalition Senator Eric Abetz, 2019, speaking against gender equality quotas in the Liberal Party. Full quote: 'Look at the Labor side of the Parliament and you can see what quotas do and it ain't a good look.'
23 Channel 7AFL, apologising for removing a photograph of Tayla Harris kicking a football from their Twitter feed rather than dealing with the trolls commenting on the thread. The original act of removal won them the Sport Silver Ernie, 2019.
24 Bettina Arndt, 2019. See note above.
25 More of Channel 7AFL's Tayla Harris apology. See note above.
26 Steve Dickson, Queensland One Nation leader, visiting a strip club in Washington DC, 2019.
27 Scott Morrison, referring to Julian Assange supporter, actress Pamela Anderson, 2019. Full quote: 'I've had plenty of mates who've asked me if they can be my special envoy to sort the issue out with Pamela Anderson'.
28 Senator Barry O'Sullivan, 2019. Full quote: 'I am going to declare my gender today, as I can, to be a woman, and then you'll no longer be able to attack me'.

Simmer down

29 Tony Smith, Qld Liberal MP, 1998.
30 John Howard, Prime Minister, 2007, on the suitability of a semi-naked burlesque act at a government climate change conference.
31 Ron Casey, Broadcaster, 2002.
32 'Magistrate #1', 1999.

33 Ron Gething, Perth Magistrate, 1996, finding a man not guilty of stalking a woman for seven years.
34 Tom Percy, QC, NSW Barrister, argued in 2002 that 6 teenagers convicted of gang-raping a young woman should not be jailed because 'they acted in accordance with the prevailing culture of the racing industry'.
35 Justice Kennedy, Court of Criminal Appeal, on the first ever child-sex-tourism case, 2002.
36 The Gold Coast Bulletin, 2002.
37 Eddie McGuire, Collingwood Football Club president, 2004.
38 PP McGuinness, Fairfax columnist, 1995.
39 Judge John Ewen Bland, Victorian County Court, 1994.
40 Judge Nigel Clarke, WA District Court, 1998, giving a two-year suspended sentence to a man for sexually abusing his 12-year-old stepdaughter.
41 Justices Crockett and Teague, Victorian Supreme Court, 1995, on reducing the sentence of a man who had admitted raping and imprisoning a woman.
42 Chris Papadopoulos, lawyer, during a rape trial in 2006, arguing that the rape was 'only brief' and 'at the very bottom end of the scale of seriousness'.
43 Barrister Ian Harrison, president of the NSW Bar Association, 2004, justifying the lack of senior women lawyers.
44 Rolf Driver, Federal Magistrate, 2005, ruling that forcing a woman to wear a miniskirt at work was not sexual harassment.
45 Eddie McGuire, Collingwood Football Club president, 2004.

GO AWAY

46 Senator David Leyonhjelm via email in 2018 to Elizabeth Donelan, who wrote to him to take exception to his comments defending Donald Trump's admission of sexual assault ('He is a man of his times, perhaps. So perhaps you could cut him a little bit of slack.') https://www.smh.com.au/opinion/australias-nastiest-most-sexist-politician-david-leyonhjelm-is-a-disgrace-to-his-office-20161021-gs7th8.html
47 Pat Caldwell, Byron Bay Magistrate (to a female defendant), 1996.
48 Noel Crichton Browne, Liberal Senator (to a female journalist), 1997.
49 Former Labor Senator Sam Dastyari was quoted in August 2018 as saying, when comparing his Channel 10 show *Disgrace!* to *Trial By Kyle*, 'After watching the clip of Kyle's show, I think what we really need is more tits' https://www.smh.com.au/entertainment/celebrity/the-goss-sam-dastyari-needs-to-wash-his-mouth-out-with-soap-20180816-p4zxyw.html
50 Andrew Fraser, NSW National Party MP, to NSW Minister for Small Business, Sandra Nori, 2002.
51 Corrinne Barraclough in *The Daily Telegraph*, 1 Dec 2017. https://www.dailytelegraph.com.au/news/opinion/corrine-barraclough-sex-scandals-or-power-trip/news-story/3b617ae801b0d7d30465d05f42289e02
52 South Sydney Presbyterian Church Spokesperson, 2007.
53 Paul Reynolds (barrister), in 2004, to his client, referring to her breasts.
54 Liberal Democrats Senator David Leyonhjelm to Greens Senator Sarah Hanson-Young, on the floor of the upper house during a division on a motion about arming women with tasers to combat violence, 28 June 2018. https://www.theguardian.com/australia-news/2018/jun/28/david-leyonhjelm-sarah-hanson-young-senator-stop-shagging-men-womens-safety-debate
55 Jamie Faulkner, *Sydney Morning Herald* Metro Liftout, 1998.

56 Ken Callander, Racing Commentator, 1996.
57 Barnaby Joyce, referring to his daughters during campaigning on the Same-Sex Marriage plebiscite.
58 *Zoo Weekly* interviewing Nikki Webster, May 2006, in response to her statement 'I want to stay true to myself. It's all about progression.'

There does come a time

59 Peter Black, NSW Labor MP, 2001 to Leader of the Opposition Kerry Chikarovski.
60 Don Talbot. Australian swimming coach (on swimmer Sam Riley), 1998.
61 Michael Costa, NSW Labor Council Secretary (aged 43), on Sharan Burrow (aged 45) running for president of the ACTU, 2000.
62 Sen. David Leyonhjelm on Sen. Sarah Hanson-Young, 2018 (as reported in a Sky News Outsiders caption 'Sarah Hanson Young is known for liking men. The rumours about her are well-known'). https://mumbrella.com.au/outsiders-presenters-apologise-for-handling-of-leyonhjelms-attack-on-sarah-hanson-young-526890
63 Jason Yat-Sen Li, Republican Movement Campaigner, on Jodhi Meares' refusal to launch the campaign T-Shirts, 2000.
64 Ray Hadley, broadcaster, on Germaine Greer at 63, 2002.
65 Grant Birse, Netball Australia marketing manager, 2006, referring to commentator and former Australian test player and captain Anne Sargeant ('old and detrimental' to the game).
66 In 2003 Fairfax columnist Alan Ramsay called veteran political commentator Michelle Grattan the Press Gallery's 'ageing blue-heeler'.
67 Paul Kent, *Daily Telegraph* (on Germaine Greer) in 2007.
68 Channel Ten executives (sacking 41-year-old news reader Tracey Spicer in 2007).

Folly

69 Kirk Pengilly (former INXS band member), 2018 https://www.smh.com.au/entertainment/former-inxs-star-kirk-pengilly-says-he-misses-slapping-a-woman-on-the-butt-20171130-gzwd06.html
70 Sen. David Leyonhjelm, during an appearance on Sky News' *Outsiders* program, interviewed by Rowan Dean and Ross Cameron, 1 July 2018.
71 Mark Latham, Federal Labor MP, 2002.
72 Mark Patrick, Advertising Agent, 1997.
73 John Justice, President of the Campbelltown Branch of the Young Liberals, 1997.
74 Mel Gibson, actor, 2006.
75 Paul Keating, former Prime Minister, 2007.
76 John Phillips, Pensioner, 2002, who unsuccessfully sued the NSW Attorney General for harm inflicted on him by up to 100 women in government departments.
77 I do not permit a woman to teach is composed, with kind permission, from the text of the article 'Things That Male Academics Have Said To Me' by Susan Harlan (http://avidly.lareviewofbooks.org/2017/11/20/things-that-male-academics-have-said-to-me/), and the comments below it, spliced with Bible verses on the position of women as teachers (1 Timothy 2:11-15; 1 Corinthians 14:34-35; Titus 2:3-5—all from the English Standard Version).

Solving the problem

78 The Bible, Genesis 2:18. All Bible quotations used in this poem are from the English Standard Version (ESV).
79 Genesis 3:16 ESV.

80 Ross Cameron on Sky News' *Jones & Co.* program, 5 Dec 2016.
81 Proverbs 12:4 ESV.
82 Robert Rabbidge, Campbelltown Magistrate, dismissing charges against a man who head-butted his girlfriend in a pub, 1999.
83 Magistrate Michael Barko won the 2018 Judicial Ernie for describing a domestic assault charge as 'a lower-end allegation that happens in every second house' and accused the woman complainant of 'slapping the court in the face' for failing to attend a hearing.
84 Proverbs 11:16 ESV.
85 Coopers Hotel Newtown social media post (and joint silver Ernie winner, 2018). The full post was 'Keep calm and slap a bitch as we approach the finals of this year's NRL!'.
86 Proverbs 21:19 ESV.
87 Keysar Trad, President of the Australian Federation of Islamic Councils, on Andrew Bolt's radio show in Feb 2017. Trad later apologised for his 'clumsy' comments.
88 Ephesians 5:22-24 ESV.
89 One Nation candidate Mark Thornton's business (a sex shop) posted to its Facebook page in November 2017 that 'Good sex should be in the gray (sic) area between "tickle fight" and domestic violence'.
90 1 Corinthians 11:8-9 ESV.
91 Mark Latham on his 2MMM podcast, 22 Jan, 2016. https://www.abc.net.au/news/2016-01-22/mark-latham-under-fire-for-triple-m-podcast-domestic-violence/7107650
92 Proverbs 21:9 ESV.
93 Mark Latham, *loc cit.*
94 Peter Nagle, NSW Labor MP, 1994, referring to male perpetrators of domestic violence.
95 Mark Latham, *loc. cit.*
96 Proverbs 19:13 ESV.

Strong Advice

97 (Federal) National Party Senator Barry O'Sullivan, Senator for Queensland, July 18 2017 in an interview with BuzzFeed News. Further quotes from Senator O'Sullivan in this interview appear throughout the poem.
98 Lyrics of the song 'Billie Jean', by Michael Jackson, © 1982 ('Thriller' album) The Estate of Michael Jackson. Further excerpts from the lyrics appear throughout the poem.
99 Text of Resolution 26, a proposed anti-abortion amendment to the Liberal / National Party Coalition of Queensland Policy Platform, in support of which Senator Barry O'Sullivan spoke at length. As reported by Gina Rushton, BuzzFeed, 18 July 2017.
100 Text of Resolution 26.
101 Australian Greens Senator Larissa Waters, during debate in the Australian Senate on Mon 12 Nov, 2018.
102 **r e   me   mber 2017** is an erasure of Don Burke's public statement of 26 November 2017. Mr Burke made his statement in response to a joint ABC-Fairfax News story alleging he had sexually harassed staff on the Nine Network television program *Burke's Backyard* over a number of years. For more information see this news story: http://www.abc.net.au/news/2017-11-27/don-burke-accused-of-sexual-harassment-indecent-assault/9188070

103 **Total fabrication** is a cut-up composed solely of words and phrases from Don Burke's public statement of 26 November 2017. See previous note.
104 **Two-hole blues**: 'Two-hole' is a violently misogynist slang term for 'woman'. All material in the first 6 stanzas of this poem is sourced from the Random Rape Threat Generator at http://rapeglish.com/, a resource compiled by academics Dr Emma A Jane (UNSW) and Dr Nicole Vincent (Macquarie University, UNSW) from hundreds of real-life misogynist messages involving death or rape threats, and/or particularly sexually explicit rhetoric, collected over a period of 18 years. The peculiar misogynist idiom used to make these threats, christened 'Rapeglish', can be broken down into the following interchangeable components: *Salutation – adjective + noun - punctuation (optional) - transitional phrase - outcome part 1 - outcome part 2*. In order to avoid any prosecution for making actual violent death threats, the 'outcomes' are almost always expressed as either (a) orders for the recipient to do something of her own accord which will result in violence to her; or (b) 'hopes' that something violent will happen to the recipient. In the poem, all the misogynist statements have been changed from the second to the first person to underscore this feature of Rapeglish. See further Jane, Dr Emma A, *Misogyny Online: a Short (and Brutish) History (*Sage, 2017).
105 **Supreme gentleman** was created from the transcript of Elliot Rodger's video 'Retribution'. Rodger uploaded the video to YouTube on May 23 2014. The following day he took a firearm to a sorority house in Isla Vista, California and opened fire, murdering six people and seriously injuring 13 others before turning the gun on himself. His actions made him somewhat of a hero to lonely men in the self-styled 'incel' ('involuntarily celibate') community (Clementine Ford, *Boys Will Be Boys,* Allen & Unwin, 2018, pp 193-198). Transcript sourced from the *LA Times* May 24 2014: http://www.latimes.com/local/lanow/la-me-ln-transcript-ucsb-shootings-video-20140524-story.html. The text was then manipulated using the heroku glass leaves text manipulation app at http://glassleaves.herokuapp.com/ (in particular, the 'get nouns and adjectives' manipulation).
106 **Only fair** was also created from the transcript of Elliot Rodger's video 'Retribution' (see previous note). The text was then manipulated using the heroku glass leaves text manipulation app at http://glassleaves.herokuapp.com/ (in particular, the 'create Markov chain' manipulation, which works a little like predictive text on a mobile phone).
107 **Eurydice's Last Sky** is based on the constellation of Virgo as seen from the southern hemisphere during our winter. Each stanza corresponds to a star in the constellation. Virgo was prominent above Melbourne on 13 June 2018, at the time of the murder of comedian and writer Eurydice Dixon. The events in the poem are based on news reports of the murder and subsequent statements by authorities. This poem was exhibited as an artwork (with the stanzas placed in their constellation positions on the body of a black dress) in the Belconnen Arts Centre exhibition 'Postcards from the Sky', Feb 8-Mar 17, 2019.

THE NIGHT BOOK

Julia after Tony's boning: The orator Cicero was, at the time of his assassination in 44BC, the most powerful public speaker and debater in the Roman world, and had directed many of his most devastating polemics at Marc Antony. Roman historian Dio states that after death, Cicero's head and hands were removed and set to be displayed on the speaker's platform in the Forum, but before being taken there the head was first delivered to Marc Antony at home, whereupon 'Antony uttered many bitter reproaches against it ...[a]nd [his wife] Fulvia took the head into her hands before it was removed, and after abusing it spitefully and spitting upon it, set it on her knees, opened the mouth, and pulled out the tongue, which she pierced with the pins that she used for her hair, at the same time uttering many brutal jests.'—Cassius Dio, *Roman History* 47, 8, as quoted in 'Unsexing Fulvia' by Suzanne Dixon http://dangerouswomenproject.org/2016/07/19/unsexing-fulvia/. See also Beard, Mary, *Women and Power,* Profile Books (London, 2017) pp 43, 102 and https://lydiaslibrary.wordpress.com/2014/10/02/ciceros-tongue/.

Ba by Joy is an erasure of a media statement made by then-deputy Prime Minister Barnaby Joyce on 13 Feb 2018, about his personal life. Film of the second half of the speech can be viewed here: https://www.theguardian.com/australia-news/video/2018/feb/13/barnaby-joyce-makespublic-apology-to-family-partner-and-voters-video. Joyce was also one of the loudest voices in Australian politics calling for the same-sex marriage plebiscite of 2017, even when other Coalition members and his own Prime Minister were equivocal. See for example: 'Nationals leader Barnaby Joyce won't compromise, he wants plebiscite', by Matthew Killoran, *The Courier-Mail,* September 26, 2016 https://www.couriermail.com.au/news/queensland/nationals-leader-barnaby-joyce-wontcompromise-he-wants-plebiscite/news-story/afab1e4ed966765e31204df5dbc36d37.

22 November 2018 is composed of found text from the Bible (English Standard Version - Matthew, Romans, and Corinthians), and from the following online news articles, in particular headlines, captions of photographs and photographic 'alt-text': https://www.abc.net.au/news/2018-11-22/isolated-tribesmen-kill-american-on-remote-indian-island/10520806; https://www.abc.net.au/news/2018-11-26/police-struggling-to-remove-body-from-north-sentinel-island/10553704; https://www.abc.net.au/news/2018-11-22/how-can-the-sentinelese-people-stay-away-from-the-outside-world/10521126.

FUGAL STATES

in/sight, after a photograph by Ann Balla (1939-2012), was commissioned by Red Room Poetry and the Art Gallery of NSW in response to the exhibition 'Shadow catchers: Shadows, body doubles and mirrors at play in photography and the moving image', 2020.

Phrases in italics in the poem **Marks** are quotes from Bligh, William, MS 5393-Notebook and list of mutineers, 1789 [manuscript]./Item 2, p 1, held in the National Library of Australia: https://nla.gov.au/nla.obj-233730330/view

VENTRILOQUIES

All translations in this section are by Melinda Smith, with the assistance of Dr Rina Kikuchi and Kawaguchi Harumi (Japanese) and Michael Teece (Latin). 'Map of the peninsula' and Welcome Home' were first published in English in *Poet to Poet, Contemporary Women Poets from Japan*, edited by Rina Kikuchi and Jen Crawford (Recent Work Press, 2017).

Two poems by Sulpicia: Sulpicia, a rare woman poet writing in Latin, lived in the reign of Augustus (27 BC—AD 14). She is believed to be the author of six short poems (some 40 lines in all) included in the corpus of Tibullus's poetry (poems 3.13-18). These translations were presented as part of a public program of Latin poetry at the National Museum of Australia's 'ROME: City and Empire exhibition', Nov-Dec 2018. Many thanks to Michael Teece for his word-for-word translations. I also consulted Anne Mahoney's translations of the same poems.

Original Latin of Sulpicia 5 (Tibullus 3, 17=4.11):

> Estne tibi, Cerinthus, tuae pia cura puellae,
> > quod mea nunc vexat corpora fessa calor?
> A ego non aliter tristes evincere morbos
> > optarim, quam te si quoque velle putem.
> At mihi quid prosit morbos evincere, si tu
> > nostra potes lento pectore ferre mala?

Original Latin of Sulpicia 6 (Tibullus 3, 18=4.12) :

> Ne tibi sim, mea lux, aeque iam fervida cura
> > ac videor paucos ante fuisse dies
> si quicquam tota commisi stulta iuventa
> > cuius me fatear paenituisse magis,
> hesterna quam te solum quod nocte reliqui,
> > ardorem cupiens dissimulare meum

Pairs first published in Japanese as '*Kutsu*' in *Yoi Hikari* (*Benevolent Light*), Nanarokusha, 2016.

Map of the peninsula first published in Japanese as '*Hantō no chizu*' in *Hantō no chizu* (*Map of the Peninsula*), 2009; first published in English in *Poet to Poet, Contemporary Women Poets from Japan*, edited by Rina Kikuchi and Jen Crawford (Recent Work Press, 2017).

Welcome Home first published in Japanese as '*O-kaeri*' in *Hantō no chizu* (*Map of the Peninsula*), 2009; first published in English in Kikuchi and Crawford, *op. cit.*

Sweet nothing first published in Japanese as '*Kōrizatō o kuwaeru*'.

21 buttons for Yoshiko (an original work, not a translation) was commissioned by the National Museum of Australia, June, 2019, for the 'Collections and Verse: Studio Objects' project.

Arthur Calwell, quoted in the *Argus*, 10 March, 1948, rejecting the first official application from an Australian serviceman to marry a Japanese bride (made in October 1947 by Corporal H.J. Cooke).

Acknowledgements

Thanks to the editors of the following publications, where several of these poems first appeared: *Axon: Creative Explorations, Backstory Journal, Cordite, DUSIE, Erase the Patriarchy (US), Island, Meanjin, Meniscus, Not Very Quiet, Other Terrain Journal, Rabbit, Southerly, The Canberra Times, Verity La, Westerly,* and the Recent Work Press publications *Listen, bitch* (2019; with Caren Florance), *Giant Steps* (2019), *Abstractions* (2018), *Poet to Poet*: *Contemporary Women Poets from Japan* (2017), and *Metamorphic: 21st Century Poets respond to Ovid* (2017). Thanks also to the National Museum of Australia, Red Room Poetry and the ACT Government, for commissioning poems that appear in this collection, and to the Belconnen Arts Centre for exhibiting two of them as part of artworks in the 'Postcards from the Sky' Exhibition (February - March 2019), curated by Lizz Murphy.

Thanks to ArtsACT for the generous grant which enabled me to write the book.

Additional thanks are due to the Neilma Sidney Literary Travel Fund and the Myer Foundation for assisting with the trip to Japan in July 2018 which made possible the translation of Harumi Kawaguchi's poem 'Sweet nothing' and Mizuki Misumi's poem 'Pairs'. For all the Japanese translations, many thanks to Dr Rina Kikuchi of the University of Canberra, the Australian National University and Shiga University, and to Dr Jen Crawford of the University of Canberra. Many thanks also to Harumi Kawaguchi for much discussion and assistance, and to Mizuki Misumi for permission to translate her work.

As always, much gratitude to Martin Dolan, Suzanne Edgar and Michael Thorley for their comments on most of these poems. Extra thank-yous go to Matt Hetherington for many discussions about the 'Listen, bitch' and 'The space inside his fist' poems, to Penelope Layland for her sensitive editing, and to the eternally indefatigable Shane Strange, publisher at RWP.

About the author

Melinda Smith is a poet, editor, teacher, arts advocate and event curator based in Canberra. She is the author of seven other poetry collections, including the 2014 Prime Minister's Literary Award-winner *Drag down to unlock or place an emergency call*. She frequently collaborates with artists in other disciplines including dancers, musicians and visual artists, and is also a former poetry editor of *The Canberra Times*. She lives and writes in the ACT, on Ngunnawal country.

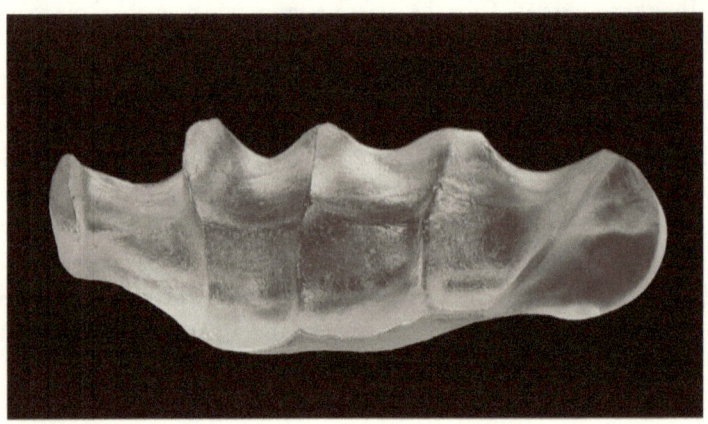

The cover image features Neil Roberts, *The Space Inside My Fist*, 1995, 9.8 x 3.4 x 3.4 cm (irreg.). Lead crystal edition of 20 created by Luna Ryan at Canberra Glassworks in 2017, cast from terracotta original. Photograph: David Paterson. © Neil Roberts/Copyright Agency, 2020. Reproduced with permission.

www.ingramcontent.com/pod-product-compliance
Lightning Source LLC
Chambersburg PA
CBHW020327010526
44107CB00054B/2005